four caliphates

the formation and development of the islamic tradition

• • • ellipsis

four caliphates

the formation and development of the islamic tradition

First published 1998 by
●●●ellipsis
2 Rufus Street
London
N1 6PE
EMAIL ...@ellipsis.co.uk

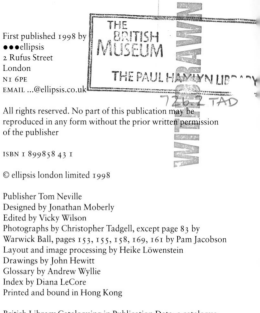

ISBN 1 899858 43 1

Publisher Tom Neville
Designed by Jonathan Moberly
Edited by Vicky Wilson
Photographs by Christopher Tadgell, except page 83 by
Warwick Ball, pages 153, 155, 158, 169, 161 by Pam Jacobson
Layout and image processing by Heike Löwenstein
Drawings by John Hewitt
Glossary by Andrew Wyllie
Index by Diana LeCore
Printed and bound in Hong Kong

British Library Cataloguing in Publication Data: a catalogue
record for this publication is available from the British Library

contents

I **Jerusalem, Temple Mountain** (early 19th-century lithograph by David Roberts).

Crowning the mount is the Dome of the Rock, the earliest surviving Islamic building, which enshrines the place where Muhammad ascended to heaven.

The major legacy of the Romans to the future of architecture was space – not just the ability to cover it, but to mould it with poured concrete. There were two main heirs: Christianity and Islam. The architects of Constantinople – capital of the Byzantine empire which survived the fall of Rome by almost 1000 years – took the Roman tradition to its apotheosis in the Christian church as the image of the City of God. The Arabs who launched Islam, with a limited tradition of settlement behind them as they moved into existing urban civilisations, pressed the architects – and buildings – of their predecessors into their service, and their architectural tradition was formed as quickly as the empire of the faith itself. They converted churches – as they converted Christians – but for several centuries it was rare that they sought to cover vast spaces anew. In the heartlands of Arabia, where the faith was born, as in its earliest conquests, the climate allowed the majority of the faithful at prayer to be left uncovered or to be covered temporarily with canopies in the courtyard. But the domains of Islam were to be extensive and in its European conquests – the Balkans in particular – the severity of the climate made cover essential. There

8

the influence of Rome, exercised through Byzantium, was direct and immediate.

Muhammad and his mission

The dramatic career of Islam began with the mission of the Prophet Muhammad, who was born into the Quraish tribe at Mecca c. 570 and died there in 632.[2] A practical man who claimed no power of intercession with God and disclaimed the miraculous, he is

2 **Mecca, the Ka'ba and its sanctuary** (17th-century Turkish miniature).

The goal of Muslim pilgrimage, the black-canopied Ka'ba was originally a tent-like pavilion with a flat roof supported by six columns, standing for the first building dedicated to God, by Abraham's son Isaac at the site of his salvation (Abraham was to sacrifice his son to God, but God sent a lamb instead). Later in the 7th century the precinct was developed as the pre-eminent place of worship (mosque derives from *masjid*, meaning place of prostration) in Islam. The concept of the sacred compound, walled to exclude all but the select (and perhaps the scene of prostration as part of devotion) dates back at least to the ancient Semitic sanctuaries of Mesopotamia.

acknowledged by his followers to have been the hand with which God wrote his definitive Word. Muslims (believers) acknowledge him to be the last in the Judaic prophetical lineage descended from Adam through Christ, and they acknowledge Christ – but not as the son of God. To them, the earlier prophets were inspired by God; God dictated to Muhammad.

Paganism was in retreat from monotheism in 6th-century Arabia: from Christianity in the north, Zoroastrianism in the north-east and Judaism in both Palestine and Ethiopia, to which Jews had fled from the depredations of Nebuchadnezzar. The inhabitants of Mecca, the reputed site of Abraham's aborted sacrifice of his son Isaac, felt these last most. A merchant who had travelled extensively in the area and was used to dealing with other travellers, Muhammad seems first to have been bent on reviving the faith of the Jewish patriarch. He received the first revelations, affirming the unity of God and the finality of his own prophethood, while in retreat: these were written. Later ones were delivered through him in a trance-like state and transcribed.

The Prophet was constrained to confide only in his closest relations as he foresaw accusations of insufferable arrogance, at least, countering his claim to be the hand and mouth of God. Headed by his wife Khatijah and his closest companion Abu Bakr, his following was considerable by 616 and he embarked on public preaching at their instigation. Rejected in his birthplace, in 622 he took refuge in Medina,[3] where the citizens were more sympathetic to his cause. From there he answered the Meccan challenge with a compilation of his revelations, later enshrined in the Muslim holy book: the Koran.

After many vicissitudes, the faithful won the right of pilgrimage to Muhammad's birthplace. Their faith infiltrated Mecca and then they invaded in force. The opposition surrendered and the Prophet returned triumphant to his native city just before his death. Miraculously translated to Jerusalem, he reputedly ascended into heaven from the rock of the Temple Mountain (Mount Moriah).[1]

Expansion and schism

Arabia was converted within two years of the Prophet's death,[4] and Islam rapidly spread into the Palestinian heartland of the Judeo-Christian tradition. A largely Arab army of the Byzantine emperor Hera-

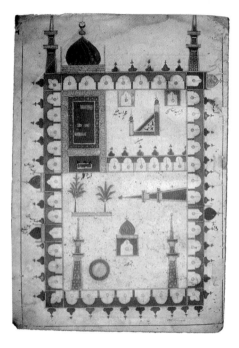

clius (610–41) was subverted and decisively defeated at Yarmuk, and Damascus was taken soon afterwards in 636. Jerusalem followed two years later. The Sassanians were defeated at Kadisiya and their capital, Ctesiphon, was taken in 637. Most of Iraq submitted before the year was out and most of Iran followed over the next 20 years. Egypt was invaded in 639 and Alexandria surrendered in 642.

The faith spread like wildfire through Egypt and along the north coast of Africa – through the zeal of the Arab conquerors, followed by equally zealous settlers, and because the Berber tribes roaming the area

3 **Medina, the Prophet's mosque** (17th-century Turkish miniature).

The courtyard, partially surrounded by verandahs and with chambers to its south, archetypal in much of the Middle East, originally formed the Prophet's house. The identity of the domestic court and the religious sanctuary was not merely fortuitous in a society that made no distinction between religious and secular life.

4 OVERLEAF **Sana'a, Yemen** view with Friday mosque centre.

preferred it to Christianity. By 720 it had taken Spain and was soon pressing up into France: in the latter its triumph was ephemeral, in the former it was sustained for centuries. East from Iran it conquered Sind in 711. Muslim colonies were established in India from the 8th century, but Islam was not a substantial force in the sub-continent until after the Delhi sultanate was established in 1190. From India Islam crossed with commerce to overwhelm the Buddhist and Hindu kingdoms of the East Indies.[5] From Iran it passed along the great trade route known as the Silk Road to China, but it was never to be predominant there.[6]

Muhammad had preached a doctrine in which there was no distinction between religious and secular life. He was the head of the body of the faithful. After his death, his principal companions in tribal council appointed in turn as caliph – *khalifa*, 'successor' to supreme authority – four of his Quraish tribal kins-

5 **Brunei, Omar Ali Saiffudin mosque** 1958, view over riverine village.

As here on the north coast of Borneo, the mosque is the centre of the community throughout the Malay peninsula and the main islands of the great Indonesian archipelago.

6 **Xian, great mosque** prayer hall.

Marking the advent of Islam in imperial China, the original T'ang foundation has been rebuilt and extended several times but always in the indigenous style.

men related to him by marriage: Abu Bakr (632–34), Muhammad's companion on the flight to Medina, father of his wife A'isha and his designated successor; Omar (634–44), father of another of Muhammad's wives and Abu Bakr's designated successor; Othman (644–56), a member of the Umayyad clan and a son-in-law of the Prophet, appointed by a Meccan tribal council and killed for venality by Medinian rebels; and Ali, husband of the Prophet's daughter Fatima, appointed by the rebels but opposed by Othman's Umayyad kinsman Mu'awiya, governor of Syria.

The rival claims of Ali and Mu'awiya, contested in indecisive fighting, were submitted to hardly more decisive arbitration. Ali's forces were revolutionary in origin and the most fanatical rejected him for agreeing to human arbitration in a matter that was for God alone to decide. The governor of Syria, with conservative tribal backing and a disciplined army, gained the upper hand and was acclaimed in Jerusalem in 660. Ali was assassinated the following year and his death perpetuated schism.

The minority (*Shi'ite*, the 'party' of Ali), swelled by converts from the ancient realms of Babylonia and Persia with their tradition of quasi-divine kingship, maintained as an article of faith that the caliphate was God-given and not open to human arbitration or appointment. For them the only line of legitimate succession as imam (leader) lay with the descent of the Prophet's blood through his daughter and son-in-law: most were to recognise 12 imams, the minority seven, and both (Ithna'ashariyyas and Isma'ilis respectively) await the second coming of their last, lost leader.

Submitting to Mu'awiya, the Arab majority (*Sunni*, the 'path' of tradition) constituted the orthodox faction which maintained their tribal practice of appointment to leadership. Yet Mu'awiya recognised that tribal election to the leadership of a rapidly expanding empire was impractical and that his power, like that of his imperial predecessors, lay with the army. Able and magnanimous, before he died in 680 he secured a general oath of allegiance to his son Yasid.

The Koran and its requirements

The central dogma on which Islam indisputably rests concerns the unity of God (Allah) and the finality of Muhammad's prophethood. The essence of God is inapprehensible and knowledge of him depends upon the 99 names he gives himself in his revelations to

Muhammad. These are enshrined the Koran. In addition there is the Tradition (*hadith*), built around the Prophet's collected sayings and accounts of his life (*sunna*). The *hadith* provides guidance but, as the book of law, the Koran imposes the conditions for submission (*islam*) and defines the consequent moral obligations of the believer (*muslim*): the 'five pillars' of Islam. These are the affirmation of the creed ('There is no god but Allah and Muhammad is His apostle'); prayer five times a day; fasting for the month of the revelation of the Koran (Ramadan, the ninth month of the lunar calendar); the giving of a prescribed proportion of income (at least) as alms to the faith and the poor; and pilgrimage to Mecca (*hadj*) at least once at the prescribed time of year for all able to afford it.

Of the five pillars of the faith, prayer and its requirements constitute the prime progenitor of Muslim architecture. The Koran specifies dawn, noon, evening and nightfall as the times of prayer but *hadith* distinguishes sunset and dusk. On the Muslim sabbath, Friday, noon prayer is congregational, at least for the male members of the community, to receive the moral instruction of a sermon. The service (*salat*) of prayer begins with the washing of face, hands and feet in a strictly defined manner. It includes affirmation of the creed and the recital of prescribed passages from the Koran in a cycle of prescribed positions, culminating in semi-prostration on a mat protecting the worshipper from the impurities of the ground.

While formal provision is often made for the modest area required for individual or family worship, the principal place of worship – the mosque (*masjid*) – was clearly the centre of its community of Muslims called to the congregational Friday (*jum'a*) noon prayers (*yaum al-jum'a*), hence Jum'a masjid (Friday mosque). Large enough to accommodate the considerable number of mats involved in an enclosure defending sanctity from pollution, its prototype was the ubiquitous courtyard house,[7] but in place of primitive trabeation, in its expansion[8–9] Islam acquired various monumental forms with its conquests: the Roman temenos or forum (see 10, page 30), the hypostyle hall of Egypt, Persia and China (see 6, page 18).

In defining the requirements of prayer, the Koran naturally moulded the principal Muslim building type. Its forms may have been Hellenistic in origin, but the Koran also governed their embellishment – perhaps to a degree further than intended. Idols are proscribed as

7 **Malulah, Syria, courtyard house**.

8 **Turfan, great mosque** exterior.

9 **Turfan, great mosque** interior.

A landmark in the advance of Islam to one of the few substantial oases on the section of the Silk Road which skirts the south of the Gobi desert, this mosque preserves the most primitive form of prayer hall.

the work of the devil (in chapter v, along with wine and games of chance), but the text does not necessarily extend to all representation of the animate in art – as strict Muslims have taken it to do in accordance with the dogma that only God is creator and that the creators of images of his creation are impious impostors. The resurrection of the Biblical ban on idolatory should be seen in the light of the growing significance of icons in Byzantium, just as stressing the Judaic unity of God denied Christian Trinitarianism. Moreover, as Islam rejected the conception of God in human form – central to Christianity – and listened only to the austere Word, anthropomorphic embellishment in the venerable tradition still vital in the lands first conquered by the Muslims naturally ceded to the calligraphic representation of Koranic texts. The highest form of Islamic art, calligraphy was supplemented by other stylised abstractions – geometry in particular – and flora.

The development of the mosque

On fleeing from Mecca in 622 and settling in Medina, the Prophet founded the first mosque in his own house (see 3, page 12). A verandah formed of palm trunks pro-

vided cover for a limited number of worshippers
before the main hall and a shelter for the Prophet's
homeless followers was erected opposite – ensuring
that the court would retain its social significance as
well as catering for the new religious activity.

Prayer was originally directed towards Jerusalem
but in 624 the Prophet aligned the axis (qibla) with
Mecca to distinguish the Muslim from Jew and Christian. It focused on the cubical Ka'ba (see 2, page 8) which
was indicated by a small stone cube until the Prophet's
mosque was rebuilt by the Umayyads in 706–10, when
a small niche (mihrab) was introduced. In fact this
seems to have marked the place where Muhammad
habitually stood as prayer leader, off centre, but it naturally asserted the qibla and was central to subsequent
mosques. Beside the mihrab is the pulpit (minbar) with
steps leading up to a canopied throne. Derived from
the Roman seat of judgement (like the bishop's chair
in the apse of the Christian basilica) the throne is left
vacant as the seat of absent authority – Muhammad
himself – and the prayer leader (imam) takes the top
step. Likewise, in place of the Prophet's bedroom a
room in the rebuilt mosque was endowed with a cenotaph representing his tomb.

The pre-eminence of the Prophet's mosque as a model hardly needs explaining but the accidents of survival leave the line of development from it difficult to trace. Regularised, its features reappeared immediately in the first new Muslim towns, such as Basra (635) and Kufa (637). Indeed, virtually all subsequent Friday mosques have had a court with shelter for worshippers on the qibla side and for itinerants opposite it, diversity of form resulting primarily from the treatment of the shelter. As Muslim builders followed their conquering leaders, adapting Christian and antique buildings or reusing materials pillaged from them, this shelter developed into an arcaded or colonnaded hall several bays deep, the outer range (riwaqs) usually returning around the other sides. A monumental expression of the mihrab as a domed chamber (qubba) – that is, a ciborium rather than a mere aedicule – is sometimes interpolated in the prayer hall further to distinguish the qibla. A tower was added – or kept from the church – for the broadcasting of the times of prayer and to assert the presence of Islam with a landmark. The great Umayyad mosque in Damascus well represents these formative developments and their essential eclecticism (see 10–12, pages 30–35).

The accession of Umayyad caliph Mu'awiya's son Yasid was challenged by Ali's younger son Hussein, who was recognised as imam by the Shi'ites – the elder son, Hassan, having renounced his rights. Killed in battle at Kerbala on 10 October 680, Hussein immediately became the holiest of martyrs to the Shi'ite cause, and though the debacle was due to the desertion of his erstwhile followers, opprobrium was heaped on the regime. This was to undermine it, but Umayyads reigned from Damascus for another 70 years. The most effective were Abd al-Malik (685–705) and Abd al-Walid (705–15), both of whom assiduously sustained a professional army encamped in the manner inherited by Byzantium from the Romans (see 15, page 40).

Umayyad mosques
The great mosque of Damascus was built by al-Walid. The exercise is typical of Arab practice in old urban civilisations. There had been a cult centre on the site since time immemorial: under the emperor Theodosius I (379–95) the last temple of the Roman era was converted into the church of St John the Baptist – it contained his head, as does the mosque. The Muslims demolished the former temple but kept the precinct and

the umayyad caliphate

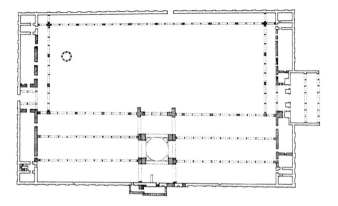

10 **Damascus, great Umayyad mosque** 705–15, plan.

The temenos of the Roman temple – 157 by 100 metres
(515 by 328 feet) – provided the prayer court and the bases
of the southern minarets (the northern one was added in the
late 10th century). There seems to have been a propylaeum

to the east but it is now obliterated. Al-Walid's builders
were responsible for the piers, originally alternating with
columns, which form the cloisters. The triple colonnade
of the prayer hall may have been inspired by the typical
basilica, Roman or Christian, with its central nave and
side aisles, but here all three parts are equal in width.
At the head of the transept which cuts through these
colonnades, the main mihrab is the earliest known,
though it was probably anticipated in al-Walid's rebuilding
of the Prophet's mosque at Medina. Two other mihrabs
were subsequently arranged in near symmetry with it in
the qibla wall, while a fourth, just to the west of the central
one, dates from after the fire which destroyed most of
the mosque in 1893. Since the mosque was a social and
political centre as well as a place of worship (Islam makes
no distinction between religious and secular life) it usually
contained the community's treasury, here a domed octagon
raised on columns towards the west end of the court.

Contemporary with the Damascene work, al-Walid's
new Aqsa mosque in Jerusalem (709–15) and reconstruction
of the Prophet's mosque in Medina (706–10), both multi-
aisled, have subsequently been much altered.

tripled the colonnade on the south (the side of Mecca) to form the prayer hall. The regular geometry of temple and basilica ordered the plan of the mosque,[10] as the reused columns ordered the elevation of prayer hall and cloister.[11] Al-Walid is also reputed to have retained Byzantine mosaicists to embellish the elevations, interior[12] and exterior. Even after the fire which devastated the mosque in 1893, some of their work survives on the central frontispiece and western portico.

The major innovation of al-Walid's Damascene architects was the cutting of the prayer-hall colonnades by a cross-axial transept which was later

11 PREVIOUS PAGES **Damascus, great Umayyad mosque** court from the north-east corner with prayer hall left, treasury right.

A dome was originally inserted over one of the bays in front of the mihrab at an unknown date, presumably after the example of the Prophet's mosque at Medina where the earliest references to such a dome follow the early 8th-century Umayyad rebuilding. The present dome is an unhappy reconstruction after the fire of 1893 on 11th-century foundations. The south-eastern minaret is reputedly based on the bell tower of the Christian cathedral.

12 **Damascus, great Umayyad mosque** prayer-hall interior.

crowned with a dome. This reinforced the central mihrab in asserting the qibla and also accommodated the prince at worship in a special enclosure (maqsura). Similarity has been seen between the court façade and the representation of a Byzantine palace in Theodoric's church of S Apollinare Nuovo at Ravenna (see volume 4, IMPERIAL SPACE, page 140). In both the central frontispiece derives from the Roman fastigium – the monumental propylaeum of temple and palace which was particularly prominent in Syria.

Caliph al-Walid's expansive predecessor Abd al-Malik was the first great Umayyad builder – indeed, he was responsible for the faith's most sacred monument after the mosques of Mecca and Medina: the Dome of the Rock in Jerusalem, which enshrines the summit of Mount Moriah where Muhammad is believed to have ascended to heaven. Crowning the site of the Temple of Solomon and dominating the holy city, it was clearly conceived to celebrate the triumph of Islam. Modelled on the centralised antique tomb or its derivative the Christian martyrium, specifically the Anastasis rotunda built by the emperor Constantine over Christ's sepulchre (see volume 4, IMPERIAL SPACE, page 172), the splendid octagonal

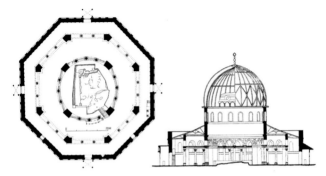

13 **Jerusalem, Dome of the Rock** 691, plan and section.
Set on a platform in the precinct of the Judaic Temple
of Solomon rebuilt by King Herod, the mosque is reached
through arcaded screens at the head of six flights of
stairs and entered through porticos facing in the cardinal
directions. The octagonal envelope is echoed in the screen
dividing off the ambulatory, but the perimeter of the
central chamber, below the double-skinned timber dome –
20 metres (66 feet) in diameter – hovers between circle
and square.

14 Jerusalem, Dome of the Rock exterior from the south
showing screen of pointed arches.

Contrary to normal Byzantine practice, the dome rises
high on its drum over the surrounding ambulatory roofs.
Its gilding enhances the impact of Islam on the holy place
of Jews and Christians. Originally covered with mosaics,
the octagonal exterior wall with its partially blind arcading

canopy is supported by arches springing from antique columns alternating with piers.[13] These form a double ambulatory for pilgrims to circulate around the holy rock and Byzantine mosaicists were retained to embellish them. The arches are generally lightly pointed: offering more resistance to the load bearing down upon it than the semi-circular form – which tends to flatten out at the top – the pointed arch was to be characteristic of Islamic architecture.[14]

Camps and palaces

The palace of the Umayyads in Damascus has disappeared but several provincial establishments remain and there is a series of well-preserved, if enigmatic, fortified compounds in the Syrian desert. Modelled on the Roman fort, indeed sometimes taken from a Byzantine

was sheathed with magnificent tiles by the Ottomans from the 16th century. However, far more of the original mosaics survive inside than in the first Umayyad mosques. These may be Byzantine in execution and in the way they ramp freely in denial of the integrity of structural forms, but not in their eclectic mix of Koranic calligraphy and royal symbols with non-figurative floral motifs.

15 **Rusafa (Byzantine Sergiopolis)** entrance to walled town.

One of a string of Byzantine fortified outposts on the Syrian frontier, founded by the emperor Justinian (527–65) and annexed by Islam, the great square compound defended the establishments of church and state as well as providing

command post,[15] they accommodated peripatetic
Arab rulers out hunting or campaigning in little more
comfort than they had previously known, and were
doubtless also garrisoned centres of rural economy.

Usually square, their walls were punctuated with
circular or polygonal towers and the twin-towered
portals of age-old royal potency – when there was a
full compliment of four of these, as at Qasr al-Hayr al-
Sharqi,[16] three were blind and purely symbolic.
Within, rooms grouped into similar apartments surrounded a colonnaded or arcaded court. On the other
hand, the seat of power was an extended complex of
several courts, housing the ruler, his entourage and the
administration: to judge from the remains at provincial Amman[17] or the district centre of Anjar,[18] Roman
influence was both direct and transmitted through the
Parthians and Sassanians.

housing and facilities for the garrison. The gate as fastigium
asserted imperial power in the time-honoured manner.

Justinian devoted considerable resources to the
fortification of the imperial frontiers. The rational plan
of Rusafa, perpetuating the ideal of the Roman camp,
was common in Byzantine military planning.

30 m
90 ft

16 **Qasr al-Hayr al-Sharqi, Syria** c.728, plans of main
and secondary enclosures.

Paired apartments (beits) were typical of Umayyad
domestic building. Here particularly grand examples flank
all four sides of the square court of the main fortified
enclosure, while small utilitarian ones surround a secondary
enclosure at the site which doubtless provided for stabling
and grain storage but has been identified (by Grabar) as the
earliest known caravanserai.

17 **Amman, Umayyad governor's palace** c. 735, court
of appearance.

Directly descended from four-iwan palace buildings like
the one at Parthian Assur, through works like the Sassanian
palaces at Firozabad and Ctesiphon (see volume 4,
IMPERIAL SPACE, pages 98–107), the central space of the
well-preserved ceremonial reception pavilion may always
have been unroofed or it may have been domed. The place
of royal epiphany was usually a domed entrance pavilion
in Roman, Hellenistic and ancient Mesopotamian palaces,
and contemporary descriptions affirm that the significance
of the dome of heaven was not lost on the Umayyads.

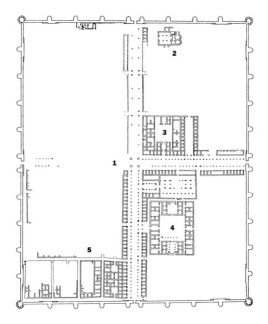

18 **Anjar, camp-city** early 8th century?, plan.

(1) Tetrapylon at the intersection of the shop-lined cardo and decumanus; (2) audience hall with attached bath house; (3) administration bulding (dar al-imara); (4) palace; (5) houses.

It is not clear from the remains how much of a garrison was quartered at Anjar, but the general distribution recalls Roman camp-cities like Timgad rather than the purely military camps like Lambaesis from which Timgad was founded (see volume 3, IMPERIAL FORM, pages 125–27). The form was sustained by the Byzantine emperors, as at Rusafa.

The administration block and palace are centred on an open court like those at other Umayyad sites – indeed, like the palaces of the Parthians, but far more regularly than in ancient Mesopotamia. Like the audience hall associated with the bath house near the northern gate, the main reception rooms on the north–south axis of the palace are enclosed basilicas rather than the Parthian or Sassanian open-ended iwan found elsewhere in Umayyad palaces. To either side of the court are matched paired apartments. The arrangement is reflected on a smaller scale and without the rigorous symmetry in the houses of the south-west quarter.

19 **Umayyad decoration** detail of western entrance of
the great mosque at Damascus.

Marble panels of exquisite quality originally provided a
high dado around the main walls. Above the marble most
exposed surfaces were covered with mosaics traditionally
attributed to artists from Constantinople. The motifs are
largely floral, realistically rendered rather than stylised,
with enigmatic buildings – the cities of the Umayyad
caliphate, the City of God? – but not people or animals.

By the end of the reign of Abd al-Walid, the empire was overextended. Advance was checked at Poitiers in central western France in 732, at Kashgar in central Asia in 736 – and before the walls of Constantinople in 717, as on several other occasions. The later Umayyad caliphs could not always rely on their armies, as their progenitors had done, and needed a civil establishment which it was beyond the Arabs to supply. Indeed, rapid expansion meant traumatically rapid change for Arab tribesmen encouraged to settle in newly conquered lands, often well-established urban civilisations with a strong sense of individual identity even when they were provinces of empires. And, of course, there was always the religious divide between Sunnis and Shi'ites.

The problems of holding the fractious elements together were enormous. In the late 740s a more than usually large and well-organised rebellion in the east was provoked by a revolutionary Shi'ite faction that preached the injustice and infidelity of the regime and the coming of a saviour (mahdi). This movement had been harnessed by descendants of Muhammad's cousin al-Abbas (566–652), who claimed primacy in Islam on the death of Ali's male heirs. Iranian

Khurasan was won over and its army, led by Yemeni Arabs, forced the governor of Iraq to flee. Yemenis throughout the empire rose in support and most of the Shi'ites rallied to the cause.

Abu'l Abbas, who had followed his brother as imam early in 749, was proclaimed caliph and assumed the title of as-Saffah – precursor of the mahdi. Seemingly invincible, his forces engaged those of caliph al-Marwan II at Busir in August 750 and prevailed. The Umayyads were decimated. One of their number, Abd al-Rahman ibn Mu'awiya, escaped to Spain and founded a kingdom at Cordova. Claiming their own back from the Abbasids, his successors assumed the title of caliph in the 10th century.

Disaffected by the elimination of their champion Abu Muslim, who had played a central role in promoting the Abbasid cause to them, the Shi'ites questioned the legitimacy of Abu'l Abbas' heir, al-Mansur (754–75) as successor to Ali, and were confronted with orthodoxy. To celebrate his dynasty's triumph – and the better to watch the Shi'ites – al-Mansur founded a new city at Baghdad, on the Tigris opposite Sassanian Ctesiphon. Baghdad was central to the great bulk of the west Asian empire, and with the

Mesopotamian tradition of imperial government to draw on the Abbasids reached the apogee of their power and prosperity there under Harun al-Rashid (786–809).

Harun's son, caliph al-Mutasim (833–42), drew on Turkish mercenaries too in his regime's constant conflict with Byzantium. Successful in war and influential in politics, their leaders soon aroused hostility in Baghdad and the caliph founded a new capital up-river at Samarra, where he fell even further under Turkish influence. Caliph al-Mutamid (870–92) moved back to Baghdad to escape the overweening power of the Turks but Turkish generals given provincial governorships under his predecessors had begun to assert their independence. The most notable was Ahmad ibn Tulun (c. 868–905), whose regime extended from Egypt to Syria in 870, though the precedent was set by the Khorasanian Aghlabids in Ifriqiya (Tunisia) before 850.

Doctrinal conflict

Turkish soldiers apart, the caliph's administration was dependent on heterodox Iran, with its own vital imperial tradition, and Iranians eclipsed Arabs in Baghdad early in the 9th century. The cultural division between Arab and Iranian was, of course, manifest most dramatically in the opposition of Sunni and Shi'ite. The five pillars of Islam were unassailable, but the sects were divided between and among themselves by differences over much else.

Strands of rationalism and emotionalism – characteristic of Sunnis and Shi'ites respectively but not exclusive to either and complementing one another on the intellectual and popular levels – lead back to the 7th century, when Islam first encountered Greek philosophy on the one hand, Christian mysticism on the other. Popular mysticism produced many saints from ascetic holy men (sufis) and orders (of dervishes housed in khanaqahs) grew up around them. Among the most significant of the intellectuals, on the other hand, were the Mu'tazilites (separatists), who denied the orthodox belief that the Koran was uncreated, asserted human responsibility in general, and challenged faith with reason.

Mu'tazilitism won the approbation of the caliphs in the first half of the 9th century, and though it was renounced by al-Mutawakkil (847–61), who persecuted its adherents as vigorously as he persecuted

Shi'ites, its intellectual rationalism remained potent. By the beginning of the 9th century the Hanafi and Maliki schools of law had emerged predominant from a plethora of contenders and, bent on reconciling their differences, the jurists Shafi'i and Hanbali founded two more from the systematic analysis of the Koran, the *hadith*, pre-Islamic convention and common practice analogous to Koranic prescription. In the following century Abu'l-Hasan al Ash'ari, a prominent Mu'tazilite who had reverted to orthodoxy, developed a systematic theology from the application of reason to the interpretation of faith. This failed to attract general approbation, of course, but inspired the founding of many theological colleges in the centres of Sunni Islam.

Rival caliphates

The lines of the great schism were redrawn in the mid 10th century when the heterodox Shi'ite Fatimids claimed the caliphate by descent from the Prophet through his daughter Fatima and her husband Ali. Their leader presented himself as the great-grandson of Isma'il al-Sadiq, great-grandson of Hussein, the second son of Fatima and Ali – though his pedigree was obscure in part. Under the banner of the mahdi, the Fatimids captured Tunisia in 909, established a new capital south of Kairouan called Mahdia and acknowledged their mahdi as caliph.

Proceeding to penetrate west and east, early in the 920s the Fatimids took Fez, capital of the independent Idrissid kingdom of Morocco founded by a refugee from the Abbasids towards the end of the 9th century. They were repulsed from Alexandria by Abbasid forces several times but, after a period of internal strife, they finally entered Cairo in 969 and went on to overcome Syria. The first two reigns were prosperous. Power had passed to the army by the 1030s but the western provinces were lost. The governor of Acre assumed control in 1074 and established a hereditary wazirate which sustained the Fatimids in Egypt for another century. By 1099, however, they had lost most of Syria to the Crusaders, come from the Christian west to free the Holy Land.

Further east the Iranian Buyids – Shi'ite, in line with traditional Iranian monarchical principles – overcame Baghdad in 945 and other Iranian regimes, like the Saffarids and Samanids, carved out concurrent kingdoms in Persia and central Asia. So too did the Ghaznavids in Afghanistan. Emasculated by exotic luxury, the Abbasids managed to subsist as puppets of various Shi'ites, but the unity of Islam, tenuous though it had long been even in western Asia, was over. Iranian powers behind the caliph's throne had little appeal in the western parts of the empire. Much of it – such as Umayyad Morocco and Spain, as we shall see – was well beyond the Abbasid writ anyway.

Abbasid cities and palaces

Caliph al-Mansur's new Baghdad was circular:[20] the centre of the Muslim world is aptly seen as the navel of the universe. Pragmatism quickly overcame the city's ideal form, however, and the caliph moved out from the centre. Nothing remains of al-Mansur's palace or mosque, but descriptions give the latter a hypostyle hall on the qibla side of a cloistered court in the tradition established by the Umayyads, and the former a court and iwan before domed chambers in the Sassanian manner.

The mosque derived from a pre-Islamic secular precedent and so too did the other building types which served the developing institutions of Islam.

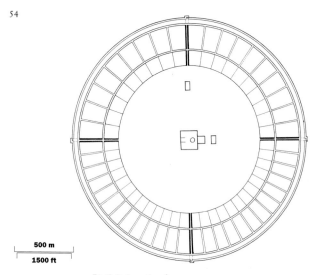

500 m
1500 ft

20 **Baghdad** c. 762, plan.

Two thousand metres (almost one and a quarter miles) in diameter, al-Mansur's City of Peace (Medinet as-Salam) was ringed by a massive wall. Four twin-towered gates, facing in the cardinal directions, had domed chambers on the first

The ubiquitous Roman camp was of inescapable importance to the expansive Umayyads (see 15, page 40). Hardly less significant was the great series of palaces from Firozabad to Ctesiphon in which 3rd- to 6th-century Sassanian rulers developed the iwan form bequeathed by the Parthians (see volume 4, IMPERIAL SPACE, pages 101–07). In the regular composition of Firozabad, which owes not a little to familiarity with the outposts of Rome, the iwan is predominant and beyond it the principal space is a domed chamber – the qubba of the four-square chahar-taq adopted for Zoroastrian fire temples. Often blind, except for the great iwans as at Ctesiphon, the richly articulated multi-storey façades are reminiscent of the Roman scenae frons (see volume 4, IMPERIAL SPACE, pages 84–85).

floor in accordance with the imperial tradition descending through Byzantium and Rome from the capitals of the Hellenistic world and, ultimately, ancient Ur. From the gates, four barrel-vaulted shopping arcades (souks) cut through rings of houses in blocks served by concentric streets and radial alleys. In the vast central area were the official buildings, the palace and the mosque.

The Muslims came into this inheritance when they
acquired Iraq. As we have seen, the palaces of the
Umayyads at Damascus have disappeared, but their
remains elsewhere seem to indicate that they capi-
talised on the legacy. The Abbasids could hardly have
avoided doing so in their turn when they established
themselves at Baghdad, in the sphere of the venerable
Mesopotamian and vital Persian cultural traditions.
If nothing remains of al-Mansur's Baghdad, the ruins
of his desert retreat at Ukhaydir and of Samarra,[21]
the capital founded by al-Mutasim in 836, clearly
reveal the influence of the Sassanians. Substantially
restored at Ukhaydir, the sequence of grand ceremonial spaces embracing vaulted halls with domed

21 **Samarra, Jusaq al-Khaqani** c. 840, plan.

Occupied for less than 50 years, the several palaces at
Samarra, 97 kilometres (60 miles) north of Baghdad, are
far less well preserved than Ukhaydir. In both the Jusaq
al-Khaqani and Balkuwara four great rectangular halls
form the arms of a cross about a central square instead of
Ukhaydir's qubba. The planning is loose in the Jusaq al-
Khaqani, much tauter in the Balkuwara – as at Ukhaydir
but on a vaster scale.

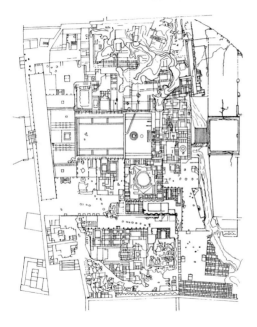

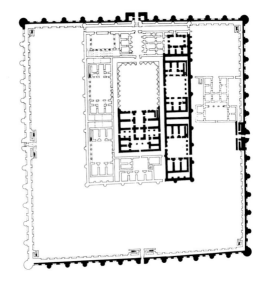

22 **Ukhaydir, palace** c. 780, plan.

The great palace at Ukhaydir, 193 kilometres (120 miles) south-west of Baghdad, is a fortified compound in the desert, like Qasr al-Hayr al-Sharqi and other Umayyad

secular works clearly inspired by Roman and Byzantine
fortified outposts (see 15–16, pages 40–42). Its context remains
obscure, as does the purpose of the irregular space between
the rectangular palace proper and the outer enclosure
– though a broad analogy has been made with the
arrangement at al-Mansur's Baghdad (see 20, page 54). Within
the main palace compound – 175 by 169 metres (574 by
554 feet) – Sassanian symmetry is disrupted only by the
placing of a mosque to the right of the entrance and guard
room. The great iwan on the southern side of the court,
higher than the flanking arcades and set in a frontispiece,
has been seen as a precursor of the pishtaq that was to
play such an important part in the later Iranian tradition.
Obviously the place of public appearance, it leads to a
similarly vaulted square chamber flanked by columned halls
and backed by a bit-hilani. If the square room was another
public audience hall, private audience would doubtless have
been held in the iwan of the southernmost apartment on the
central axis. The harem apartments to either side (recalling
the Umayyad beit) have twin iwans addressing their private
courts. Caliphate planners thus sustained the ubiquitous
Asian formula for palace planning, with its traditional
tripartite division into zones of public appearance, private
audience and harem enclosure for the royal women.

24 **Ukhaydir, palace** entrance hall.

Like the Sassanians, the Abbasids drew considerable effect from arches springing low from stumpy columns. The flattened, four-centred arch appears for the first time, perhaps, in vaulting – as here.

23 PREVIOUS PAGES **Ukhaydir, palace** view from entrance.

Surviving to roof height in several areas, the structure was restored in the 1980s. Parthian court and iwan are nowhere better represented. In Syria the Umayyads built primarily of stone supplemented by brick. In Iraq the Abbasids, like the Sassanians, relied on plastered rubble instead of stone and perpetuated the ancient Mesopotamian tradition of mud and brick.

25 LEFT **Ukhaydir, palace** private court.
The arches over the entrances from the subsidiary
courts to the private quarters introduce the incurved
horseshoe form.

26 CENTRE **Samarra, fort-palace of al-Ashiq** c. 880,
exterior with cusped blind arcading above, lobed below.
As here, cusping has been detected on the upper level
of the north wall of the main court at Ukhaydir. A decade
earlier still (c. 772), a precedent may be found in the upper
level of the gate to the fortified town of Raqqa in Syria.

27 RIGHT **Baalbek, Great Temple of Jupiter** 2nd century,
scallop-shell niche.

antechambers, a vast open court, a great iwan for public audience and a more exclusive square audience hall, is isolated by corridors from self-contained private courtyard suites.[22-23]

Decorated with plaster relief, mosaic or elaborately patterned brickwork (hazarbaf), Abbasid palaces were predominantly arcuate. Semi-circular and pointed arches – some flattened,[24] some incurved at the base like a horseshoe,[25] some fringed with semi-circular projections – appear at Ukhaydir, and much is made of the last at Samarra.[26] Multiple small-scale projections of this kind are called cusps, fewer and larger they are lobes: if the latter suggest combined horseshoes, the former seem to derive from the Roman scallop-shell niche.[27]

Abbasid mosques

Apart from primitive trabeation, multiple arcades covered the largest areas of Abbasid buildings, as in the great mosque of caliph al-Mutawakkil at Samarra.[28-29] Still overlooking its ruins is Samarra's most celebrated monument: its massive spiral minaret. Certainly not without controversy, this (and the smaller one beside al-Mutawakkil's smaller mosque at

28 **Samarra, great mosque of al-Mutawakkil** c. 850, prayer court.

The vast prayer court – 240 by 156 metres (787 by 512 feet) – is defended by two ranges of walls, the restored inner one punctuated by round towers as at Ukhaydir (see 22, page 58). Stout octagonal piers presumably supported a forest of arches over the nine-aisled prayer hall before the qibla wall (south) and cloisters (four bays deep on the eastern and western sides, three bays deep to the north).

29 OVERLEAF **Samarra, great mosque of al-Mutawakkil** spiral minaret and exterior from the east.

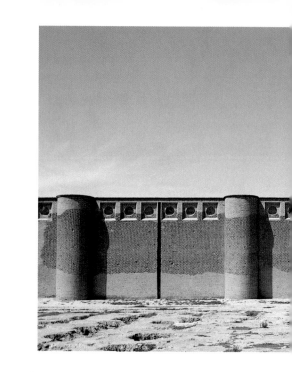

Abu Dulaf) may be seen as descending from the ancient ziggurat, specifically capitalising on the conversion of the tower of Babel – the Biblical monument to the folly of man in ceding the unity of his dominion to linguistic discord – into a base for the proclamation of the one true faith by the one true voice.

The remains of the prayer hall and cloisters within the massive walls of the great mosque – the largest in Islam – are reduced to little more than their foundations. These show the qibla bay of the prayer hall as distinguished from the others in width, like an iwan in plan at least, and the motif certainly marked the near-contemporary Abu Dulaf mosque. There, moreover, the central nave joined a double transept at right angles before the mihrab.

Some of the arches remain at Abu Dulaf, but the general effect of early Abbasid prayer-hall arcading may be gained on a much reduced scale from the Friday mosque at Nayin,[30-31] one of a provincial series in Iran. The distinction of nave and transepts recurs here, but the surface decoration is not thought to be typical of early Abbasid practice in religious building, due to the paucity of evidence for it among the ruins of Samarra.

30 **Nayin, Friday mosque, prayer hall** late 9th century,
prayer-hall court.

3 1 **Nayin, Friday mosque** prayer-hall interior with mihrab and minbar.

Carried on a variety of piers and circular and polygonal columns, the flattened arches of the prayer hall extend to three or four bays around three sides of the square court – the central ones of the eastern and western ranges raised higher than the others. A slightly wider bay in the centre of the quadruple range to the south-west asserts the qibla and there is a dome over the innermost mihrab bay. A taller arch and raised parapet in the centre of the single range to the north-east anticipate the interpolation of an iwan.

Carved or moulded surface detail of the kind shown here in stucco, predominantly stylised floral motifs confined in geometric frames or ramping within the main lines of the structure, is characteristic of early Abbasid palaces in Iraq, though the mosques there seem to have relied for their effect primarily on the play of architectural forms, particularly the scenographic vistas through multiple arcades. In so far as its dilapidation testifies, this is also the case with another mosque in the early Iranian series, at Damghan. Possibly contemporary with Nayin, it has the much more conventional arrangement of square court, three-bay prayer hall and single-bay cloisters to the other three sides. Flattened arches on plain piers address the court all round.

The development of the mausoleum

Something of the presumed severity of al-Mutawakkil's mosques may be gained from the restoration of the near-contemporary Qubba al-Sulaybiya at Samarra.[32] Certainly it is in stark contrast with the Samanid tomb in Bukhara, built less than a century later,[33-35] and related works at Tim (near Samarkand) and Isfahan, where structural forms are fragmented.[36-37] On the other hand, the decorative manipulation of structural form, apparent in the treatment of the arch in Abbasid secular building, was taken to an extreme in later Abbasid tombs: the squinch, extracted from its structural context of effecting transition from square to circle or octagon and multiplied to a reduced scale, was woven into a honeycomb-like web (muqarnas) across entire vaults. A precocious example tops the tomb of Muslim bin Quraish at Imam Dur near Samarra.[38] It is hard to imagine that the muqarnas vault sprang fully developed there, but it is presumed to be native to Iraq, if not Iran.

Islam requires burial for the dead, the body being laid flat with the face turned towards Mecca, if possible in a vaulted chamber allowing the incumbent

32 **Samarra, Qubba al-Sulaybiya** c. 862, plan and section.

Identified (not with absolute certainty) with the tomb documented as having been built for the caliph al-Muntasir (who reigned for six months in 862), this is the earliest building of the octagonal canopy tomb type to survive. Integrating square and octagon in development of the plan of the Dome of the Rock (see 13, page 37), it has a single octagonal ambulatory about a qubba. Whereas the outer arcades of the Dome of the Rock were blind, however, here the ambulatory arcades are unwalled to all sides below the dome simulating heaven.

33 **Bukhara, Samanid tomb** c. 940, plan and section.
Traditionally associated with the Samanid ruler Ismail
but probably a dynastic tomb built by Nasr (914–43), the
cube – 10 metres (33 feet) square – is a stoutly battered mass
of basket-weave patterned brickwork, relieved at the
corners by cylindrical piers and tiny stilted domes.

34 **Bukhara, Samanid tomb.**

35 **Bukhara, Samanid tomb** interior.

To support the main dome over the cubical space,
squinches effect transition from square to octagon,
colonnettes from octagon to 16-sided polygon. Unusually
the interpolation of a cross-rib in the squinches allows
for the penetration of light at the corners through the
decorative external gallery.

3 m
9 ft

36 **Tim, Arab-ata tomb** c. 977, plan and section.

The entrance arch, surmounted by three windows, is
framed by projecting bands of basket-weave brickwork and
Cufic script. The horizontal band at the top, raised higher
than the main mass by the windows, masks the dome.
Inside, instead of one arch and semi-dome across each
corner, forming an octagon over a square, a tri-lobed form
in plan and elevation consists of fragments of a lower,
broader semi-dome, springing from the corners but
decapitated and doubly recessed through rectangle and
semi-circle, supporting a taller, narrower semi-dome. The
elevation is repeated as blind arcading on the intermediate
sides. This seems to be the origin of the honeycomb-like
multiplication and fragmentation of small squinch forms
known as muqarnas.

room to sit up when called to account. The grave is marked at ground level by a recumbent stone – reflecting the position of the body below – inscribed with the 99 names of God. Strict orthodoxy left the Muslim grave open to the sky. Wishing to be buried within the orbit of 'benign influence' (*baraka*) but far from the great shrines, many endowed the graves of sufis and provided themselves with associated tomb chambers. Endowers of mosques too often had a tomb incorporated in the design after the precedent set at the Prophet's own mosque in Medina. How-

37 Isfahan, so-called Jurjir portal.

This enigmatic work, attributed to the late 10th-century Buyids, is now the gate to the Jurjir mosque – but it is unprecedented as a mosque portal if the attribution is correct. The fragmentation of the semi-dome, parallel to the fragmentation of the squinch, is furthered by cutting into it with a vertical window. Varied patterns are imposed on all surfaces: basket-weave cedes to zig-zag geometry but blind cusps fringe the main arch and within it the muqarnas-like fragments of the semi-dome are assertively framed and filled with the rectilinear stylisation of flora which begins to assimilate itself to the Cufic script below.

ever, the conquest of lands with strong traditions of
holy places and development of the heterodox Shi'ite
cult of Ali and his descendants, let alone dynastic
pretension, led to the mausoleum. A canopy was
reputedly erected over the grave of Ali soon after it
was identified and, of course, a canopy
dome enshrined the sacred rock on Jerusalem's Mount
Moriah little more than half a century after the
Prophet's apotheosis there.

Inspired by the Dome of the Rock (see 13–14, pages
37–38), the Qubba al-Sulaybiya provided one of the
two basic prototypes for the Muslim tomb: the
canopy form carried on open arches to conform con-
ceptually (at least) with *hadith* stricture that the
Muslim grave must be open to the sky. The Samanid

38 Imam Dur, tomb of Muslim bin Quraish 1085,
interior.

Over a cubical space, no longer open to the sides, there
are five tapering tiers of muqarnas. Outside, the battered
mass has circular corner piers or turrets, like the Samanid
tomb at Bukhara (see 34, page 75) but these project further like
those of several Iranian tomb towers (the slightly later ones
at Kharraqan, for instance).

tomb is the prime representative of the other type: the freestanding qubba with open arches to all four sides modelled on the Zoroastrian chahar-taq. The Arab-ata tomb at Tim introduces muqarnas and presents an early instance of an applied frontispiece (pishtaq) distinguished in height from the mass of the building, as in the contemporary Jurjir portal in Isfahan. The Imam Dur tomb is a bizarre variant of the qubba type crossed with the tower form popular in Iran. Perhaps descended from the tent, perhaps continuing the venerable antique Syrian tradition represented at Palmyra (see volume 3, IMPERIAL FORM, page 225), this variant is at its most monumental in the Gunbad-i Qabus.[39]

39 **Iran, Gunbad-i Qabus** 1006.

The earliest surviving representative of the type, this is also the largest. The severity of the brickwork, relieved only by bands of script near base and summit, is enhanced by the triangular projections radiating at ten equal intervals from the circular core. The form has a long history of increasing relief: the octagonal tower at Abarquh (1056) has a prominent muqarnas cornice.

Kairouan and Cairo

Iran apart, outside Iraq it is in Egypt and north Africa
that the most important works from the early Abbasid
period are to be found. The mosque of Amr in Fustat
(Cairo) and the great mosque at Kairouan[40–41] are
among the earliest. Built on Umayyad bases in 827 and
836 respectively, these retained the hypostyle form of
prayer hall with arches supported on a forest of reused
antique columns. The Amr mosque has been remod-
elled, but the original nucleus of the Kairouan work
survived augmentation in the later 9th century and
restoration in the 11th. Nave and transepts are defined
more lucidly here than at Samarra. A screen of horseshoe arches masks the prayer hall from the court, the
domed antechamber was transposed from Ukhaydir
to distinguish the mihrab bay, and a second dome over
the central courtyard bay, introducing the nave, con-
fronts the massive stepped minaret.[42]

   The Samarran spiral minaret (see 29, pages 66–67) reap-
pears beside the great mosque with which the Turkish
general Ahmad ibn Tulun endowed Fustat in the

40 **Kairouan, great mosque** 836 and later 9th century,
prayer hall with qibla dome.

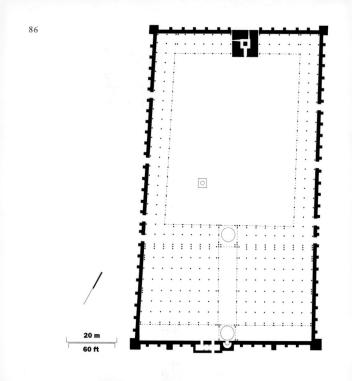

20 m
60 ft

41 **Kairouan, great mosque** plan.

Kairouan and its first mosque were founded c. 665 by Uqba ibn Nafi, the conqueror of Ifriqiya (the ancient Roman province of Africa, modern Tunisia). The present mosque was begun in self-aggrandisement by Ziyadat Allah (817–38), the Abbasids' Aghlabid viceroy who was asserting quasi-independence at the time.

Before the qibla wall (south-east), the roughly rectangular compound – 135 by 80 metres (443 by 262 feet) – has an arcaded prayer hall ten bays deep and 17 wide, the wider, higher central bay forming a nave before the domed mihrab chamber where it is joined at right angles by transepts of similar dimensions. The outer two bays are continued around the other sides of the court as cloisters. The columns supporting the arcades are mainly recycled from the province's rich heritage of Roman buildings and are screened from the court by arches on piers with attached colonnettes. Of particular importance in the richly decorated mihrab qubba is the octagonal zone of transition from square to circle with its scallop-shell squinches supporting the dome across the corners and matching cusped arches to the sides: the origin of the cusped arch in the classical scallop shell-headed niche could hardly be more clearly revealed.

42 **Kairouan, great mosque** minaret.

Hardly less arresting than its spiral counterpart at
Samarra (see 29, pages 66–67), if somewhat less plausibly
related to the ziggurat, the base of this great tiered structure
may preserve the only substantial remains of the original
mosque of Uqba ibn Nafi.

43 OVERLEAF **Fustat (Cairo), mosque of Ibn Tulun** 870s.

A square compound – c. 160 metres (525 feet) per side
and double-walled to form broad bands of communication
space as in the Ptolemaic Temple of Horus at Edfu (see
volume 1, ORIGINS, page 67) – encloses a square court (c. 92
metres/302 feet) surrounded by doubled arcades. Three
additional arcades project the prayer hall into a rectangle at
the expense of the outer channel of communication space to
the south-east (qibla). An ablution fountain occupied the
centre of the court. A mihrab marks the centre of the qibla
wall at the back of the five-aisled prayer hall.

The pointed arches, springing through a slight incurve
from columns inset into the corners of rectangular piers and
delicately incised with stylised floral motifs, are consistent
throughout.

870s,[43-44] when he ruled Egypt nominally on behalf of the Abbasids. In place of primitive trabeation or arches carried on columns, the arcades of ibn Tulun were inspired by those of Samarra – where he was a pillar of the Abbasid establishment – but set an unexcelled standard for the ordering of the haphazard collection of forms inherited from the Prophet's mosque in Medina. Prayer hall and cloisters have piers with attached colonnettes – also derived from Samarra – and pointed arches incurved at the impost.

Ibn Tulun's mosque has no dominant nave or transept. A century later, these features distinguished the al-Azhar mosque of Cairo,[45] the new centre of radical Shi'ite propaganda in the new capital of the Fatimids, who had first established themselves in Tunisia. As at Kairouan, too, the junction before the mihrab was celebrated with a domed bay. This was echoed by domed bays at either end of the transept and repeated in the centre of the courtyard range during later remodelling.

44 Fustat (Cairo), mosque of Ibn Tulun minaret.

The spiral minaret replaced an earlier one in the 14th century.

45 **Cairo, mosque of al-Azhar** c. 970, prayer hall from the court.

Though more advanced in plan than the mosque of ibn Tulun, the hypostyle prayer hall – 85 by 69 metres (279 by 226 feet) – was more conservative in elevation, with recycled columns supporting arches. These survived the remodelling of the court façades, probably in the 3rd and 4th decades of the 12th century, when the dome was built at the head of the nave.

The other great Fatimid structure, the Hakim mosque of c. 990, has domes at the ends and centre of the transept but none at the head of the nave. Piers carry its arches.

46 **Fez** view with Friday mosque centre background.

In the extreme west of the Muslim world, the Umayyads of Cordova had prospered and in the middle of the 10th century they took advantage of Fatimid problems in the east to extend their power to Morocco,[46] where unruly Berbers had undermined such unity as the Arab dynasty of the Idrissids had been able to sustain from Fez. Their apogee was reached under Abd al-Rahman III (912–61), who claimed back the title of caliph. Then Cordova was one of the most civilised cities of the world.

Decline was postponed under the weak Hisham II (976–1009) by the able vizier al-Mansur, but it was rapid thereafter. The infiltration of Berbers from north Africa unsettled the regime and a series of revolts led to the end of the Cordovan caliphate in 1031. Spain shattered into petty states whose rivalries favoured the Christians bent on reversing the tide of Islam in Iberia.

The western Umayyad rivals of the Abbasids and Fatimids ceded to none of their contemporaries as patrons of architecture – indeed, the great mosque of their capital, Cordova, is one of the chief glories of Islam.[47] Protection from the harsh winters even of southern Spain required the forest of columns supporting tiers of arches and a timber ceiling, which first

47 **Cordova, Umayyad mosque** plan as enlarged in 987.

Of the great compound – 190 by 140 metres (623 by 459 feet) – aligned north-east/south-west at radical variance from the qibla, one-third is a cloistered court, the rest a vast hypostyle hall of 17 bays brutally interrupted by the 16th-century Christian cathedral. The 11 most westerly bays (the wider central one providing a nave before the mihrab) date from the original foundation of Abd al-Rahman I (756–88) but were extended from 12 to 20 intercolumniations towards the qibla by Abd al-Rahman II (821–52). The court was given cloisters and the minaret was constructed by Abd al-Rahman III (912–61). Al-Hakam II (961–76) constructed a domed chamber beyond the central qibla bay (possibly originally intended as a maqsura for the caliph's personal use, now the Villaviciosa chapel), but this was engulfed by the addition of another 12 intercolumniations towards the qibla and superseded by three domed chambers in a screened maqsura before the new mihrab niche. Finally al-Mansur, the vizier of the last Umayyad caliph of Cordova Hisham II (976–1009), extended the prayer hall laterally towards the east by eight bays.

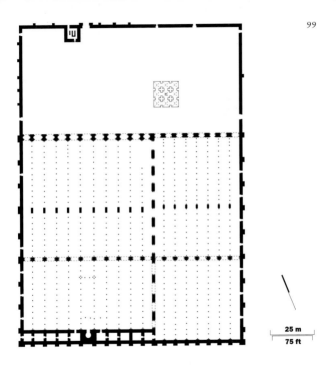

25 m

75 ft

48 **Cordova, Umayyad mosque** colonnades of 784.

The standard early Muslim practice of reusing Roman
columns as supports for a forest of arches was transformed
from the outset by the spectacular device of a second tier of
boldly accented voussoir arches springing from suspended
piers. Perhaps suggested by a Roman aqueduct, this
certainly achieved a more satisfactory relationship between
height and breadth than the available columns allowed.

49 **Cordova, Umayyad mosque** colonnades of 987.

50 **Cordova, Umayyad mosque** vault of maqsura
side bay.

51 **Cordova, Umayyad mosque** vault of mihrab bay.

Al-Hakam II's work is even more extraordinary than the
arcades of his predecessors. His maqsura screens are also
composed of superimposed arches – but of interpenetrating
cusped and horseshoe forms in three tiers. His vaults are

variations on the theme of interlocking ribs: paired in a grid
over a rectangle to form a square central compartment, but
cut by ribs linking the centres of adjacent sides to form
another square on the diagonal in the Villaviciosa chapel;
paired between opposite sides of an octagon to form an
eight-pointed star and an octagonal central compartment
in the two side bays of the definitive maqsura; overlapping
across the oblique angles between each pair of adjacent sides
of an octagon to form an octagonal central compartment in
the central bay before the mihrab.

Maximum use is made of cusped and horseshoe arches
for clerestory windows and squinches, the scalloped semi-
domes behind the horseshoe squinches of the two subsidiary
domes in the maqsura again demonstrating the origin of the
cusped arch – but on the horizontal rather than the vertical
plane. The maqsura vaults rely on the play of varied lighting
on their ribbed compartments and inset floral domelettes;
the vault of the central mihrab bay is covered in rich mosaic.

The mihrab itself is a richly decorated octagonal chamber
of marble and stucco. It is entered through an intricately
incised horseshoe arch whose exaggerated incurvature
within a rectangular frame emblazoned with Koranic script
reflects the form of the main gate to the court, as though
marking the final stage in the progression to grace.

appeared in 784 and was extended to cover much of the enclosure over the next two centuries.[48-49] Caliph al-Hakam II (961–76) was responsible for the most elaborate work: the bays of the enclosure for royal worship (maqsura), with their interlaced cusped arches, and the cross-ribbed cannelled domes finely chased with stylised floral motifs and Koranic calligraphy.[50-51] The arch had begun to lose its purely structural form at Ukhaydir: at Cordova it had become purely decorative in the incurved cusped and interlaced style which came to be called Moorish.

Palaces and retreats

Little of the caliphate palace survives in Cordova, but the incompletely excavated retreat of Abd al-Rahman III in the nearby countryside at Medinat al-Zahira, littered with lavish detail, has revealed terraces drawn from the contours of the site: apartments surrounding formal courts, formally and informally related, overlooked gardens, at least one of which was a rectangle crossed by axial canals.[52] The four-square garden (chahar bagh) is the microcosm of paradise in accordance with the ancient Persian ideal of order to which the Koran's Eden is related: an enclosed square divided

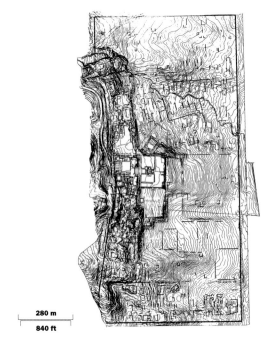

280 m
840 ft

into quarters by four rivers flowing in the cardinal directions from the source of the waters of life in the centre. And in the Koranic tradition the gardens of heaven were set with pavilions built over water. Thus Abd al-Rahman III's palace may well have been the image of the earthly paradise – as the imperial palace in Constantinople and, doubtless, Samarra's Jusaq al-Khaqani were before it.

The relaxation feasible at the apogee of Cordovan power is not typical of the earliest palace remains in the west. As in the heartlands of the Umayyad and Abbasid caliphates, these are sparse, but they tend to be regular – even axial – with a nuclear court in a stoutly defended rectangular compound. A series of

52 Medinat al-Zahira, palace of Abd al-Rahman III

founded 936, site plan.

A contemporary court chronicler records expansive views over gardens, many-columned pavilions, and fountains of bronze and marble. The excavations reveal an informal grouping of palace buildings on the top terrace overlooking the gardens. As at Samarra, the main elements of the palace were separated from one another by corridors. The complex was destroyed in the Berber revolt of 1010.

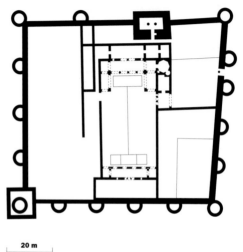

53 **Zaragoza, Aljaferia palace** c. 1050, plan.

Built for the ruler Abu Ja'far Ahmad ibn Suleim (1049–83), the Aljaferia conforms in general to the type descended from the Roman camp through the Umayyad qasr (see 16, page 42) – as did the Almohad Alcazar in Seville.

In an incompletely rectangular compound, stoutly defended against the Christians nearby, the principal apartments overlooked an arcaded court from the north and south. The parallel portico and hall to the south, relatively remote from the eastern entrance, were probably for private audience. The matching portico to the north served a variety of rooms including an octagonal mosque.

north African examples leads to the mid 11th-century
Aljaferia of Zaragoza.[53] In the embellishment of the
halls and mosque here, however, the decorative manipulation of structural form exceeds even the extreme of
late Cordova and strays into unique asymmetry.[54]

54 **Zaragoza, Aljaferia palace** mosque interior.
    The interior of the mosque was a riot of cusped and
lobed arches in interlaced frames with most surfaces
overwhelmed by intricate floral patterns incised in stucco.
The superimposition of filigree valances to arches whose
trajectory goes beyond door frames elsewhere produces
a bizarre asymmetry which was to remain unequalled
until the 18th century.

The decadent Abbasids were saved and orthodoxy was reasserted in the east in the middle of the 11th century by Turks. In the last quarter of the 10th century Seljuk, an Oghuz Turkoman tribal chief, entered his followers in the service of the Samanids as soldiers, settled them near Bukhara and converted to orthodox Islam. Challenged by Ghazni after the fall of the Samanids, Seljuk's two grandsons won control of Khurasan: Chaghri Beg consolidated his hold there; Tughril Beg set out to exterminate the Shi'ite Buyids, who still held the Abbasid caliph in their thrall. He invaded Baghdad in 1055, received the submission of the last Buyid and was given the title of sultan by the grateful caliph.

Forging a successful army from unruly tribesmen was expected of a great chief. Forging a sound administration from the same material was beyond even Tughril Beg. And immediate opposition from other Turks, particularly those who had served the Buyids as generals, received Fatimid support. Baghdad was lost, then re-won with help from Khurasan, and a

55 OVERLEAF **Isfahan** view from the Friday mosque with souks centre.

working partnership was forged between sultan and caliph: the latter providing religious authority, the former power. The caliph remained in Baghdad. The better to control dissident Shi'ite Iran, the sultan moved to Hamadan and then on to Isfahan.[55]

Tughril Beg was succeeded by Chaghri Beg's son Alp Aslan. With him from Khurasan came the great vizier Nizam al-Mulk, who reformed the caliphate's administration, coped with Turkoman occupation of arable land by establishing military fiefs which supported the soldiers in return for protection, and launched a programme of orthodox Sunni education. Meanwhile Alp Aslan launched his forces against the remaining provinces of the Byzantine empire in eastern Anatolia and northern Syria. Seljuk hold on the latter was not secured until after the accession of Malik-shah in 1072. Their conquest of Anatolia was assisted by calls for help from a rival claimant to the Byzantine throne, and by 1080 most of Asia Minor was in the hands of Seljuk rivals to Malik-shah.

Nevertheless, the Seljuk apogee was reached in Iran and Iraq under Malik-shah and Nizam al-Mulk – though the latter was assassinated in 1092 shortly before the death of the former. Dynastic discord and tribal restiveness undermined the regime and provincial governors began to assert autonomy. Sanjar, governor of Khurasan from the beginning of the new century and sultan from 1118 to 1157, restored control and revived the regime's glory but ultimately succumbed to tribal revolt. The Abbasids revived and Sanjar's last heir died in 1194.

Meanwhile, the cross-currents of fortune in the conflict of Christian and Muslim in the west led to the contraction of Seljuk Anatolia to the sultanate of Rum centred on Konya. Its peak was reached in the mid 13th century. By then, too, Muslim opposition to the Latin kingdoms established by the Crusaders in the Holy Land had reached a climax.

In the decade after 1127 the Seljuk governor of Mosul, Nur al-Din Zengi, penetrated northern Syria and captured Aleppo. Damascus was won by his followers in 1154 and his dynasty reigned there until 1181 and from Aleppo to Mosul until 1222. Nur al-Din Zengi's troops were commanded by Kurds, most notably Salah al-Din, who successfully opposed a Christian expedition to Egypt in 1169. He was made wazir by the Fatimid caliph but allied himself with the Abbasid caliph on the death of his patron in 1171. He restored the name of the Abbasid caliph to Friday prayers, terminating the Fatimid caliphate, and established his Ayyubid dynasty. After further success against the Christians, he took Syria in 1183 and the kingdom of Jerusalem in 1187.

After Salah al-Din's death in 1193, his Syrian domains disintegrated but his heirs held Egypt and reconsolidated control over Syria in 1199. With the help of an army of Turkish slaves (Mamluks) they warded off the Crusaders, who were increasingly preoccupied with eliminating the Egyptian threat. During a succession dispute in the mid century, the Mamluk leader seized the initiative and established a new dynasty.

By the middle of the 13th century Seljuks, Abbasids and almost everyone else were at the mercy of the Mongol hordes unleashed across Asia by the devastating Genghis Khan (1206–27). Northern China had fallen to his sons Ogdai and Tule by 1234. At the head of the Golden Horde, his grandson Batu had reached Moscow in 1237, Budapest in 1241. Another grandson, Hulagu, cut a swathe through central Asia to Baghdad and destroyed it on the surrender of the caliph in February 1258. Aleppo and Damascus followed in 1260 but then the carnage was stopped by the greatest of the Mamluk rulers of Egypt, Baybars. He went on to eliminate the last of the Christians in the Holy Land. Reeling from their first reverse, the Mongols turned on the Seljuks of Rum.

Most of Asia and eastern Europe was divided between the heirs of Genghis Khan. Ogdai and his successors as Great Khan (*khagan*), then Tule's successors, ruled Mongolia and China. The Golden Horde of Batu had Russia. Hulagu had the Seljuk domains and took the title of Ilkhan (subsidiary khan). His successors embraced Islam before the end of the century and the regime reached its height under Ghazan (1295–1304) and Oljeitu (1304–16). Traditional tribal rivalries undermined unity after Abu Said (1316–35) and the line was extinguished in 1353. The dynasty of Timur succeeded in 1370.

Mosques and madrasas: the four-iwan plan

Determined to reassert orthodoxy in the face of the Shi'ite challenge issued by the Fatimids, the Abbasids' great Seljuk vizier Nizam al-Mulk promoted instruction in canonical law. Teaching was always the prerogative of the mosque, but the school was usually the

56 **Mosul, traditional house** court and iwan.
Relatively modern, such houses may nevertheless
be taken as representative of a long-standing tradition.
It was in this context that the madrasa developed in Iran
and Iraq.

house of the teacher – especially when a measure of discussion was admitted to supplement rote learning. From the end of the 9th century piety and missionary zeal prompted private patrons to sponsor special collegiate buildings (madrasas) in eastern Iran: iwans accommodating the various classes doubtless interrupted cells accommodating the students around a quadrangle. The inclusion of a small mosque would have dictated orientation, but remains are too thin on the ground to indicate any formal ordering of the characteristic domestic arrangement.[56]

Neither remains nor descriptions of the earliest state-sponsored madrasas, the Nizamiyas founded by Nizam al-Mulk, indicate how far evolution was taken before the end of the 11th century. The existence of four schools of Sunni law imposed its own discipline, and an obviously relevant prototype for formal order was ready to hand in the four-iwan palace building inherited by the caliphate from the Parthians. The earliest madrasa-builders of eastern Iran may well have found another model in the Buddhist vihara – commonly a cell-bordered court dominated by a larger cell for the holy image. Extirpated by Islam, Buddhism had risen to predominance in the area under the patronage of the Kushanas, who united north-eastern India with eastern Iran and central Asia in the first three centuries of the Christian era. Following in the footsteps of the Parthians, moreover, the Kushanas were themselves no strangers to the four-iwan palace plan.

The earliest madrasa known to have been designed with four iwans specifically for the four schools of Sunni law is the Mustansiriya of Baghdad, built by the penultimate Abbasid caliph, al-Mustansir in 1233.[57-58] The Shi'ites quickly resorted to the madrasa too, but their earliest four-iwan Iranian example is 100 years later. Well before the Mustansiriya, however, the four-iwan plan had been adopted for mosques in Iraq and western Iran.

Four iwans served a novel purpose in an orthodox Sunni madrasa: they denied the distinct focus that had always been essential to the mosque, whatever the sect it served. In fact the iwan, as the traditional place of epiphany, first recommended itself as the dominant element on the qibla in Iranian mosques, asserting both entrance to the compound and entrance to the sanctuary, where the domed qubba featured in Syria, Egypt and the west.

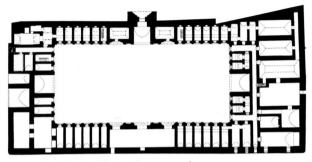

57 **Baghdad, Mustansiriya madrasa** 1233, plan.

This extensive rectangular building – 106 by 48 metres (348 by 157 feet) – with student cells on two storeys and communal facilities around a court (62 by 26 metres/203 by 85 feet) was built in emulation of the works of the great Nizam al-Mulk, who had served as caliph to al-Mustansir's ancestor 150 years earlier. The iwan of the southern range, opening through three arches, is an elongated hall which doubled as a mosque. The triple motif is echoed before three separate rooms on the northern side.

58 OVERLEAF **Baghdad, Mustansiriya madrasa** court.

Several of the earliest Persian mosques were domed qubbas inspired by – even converted from – Sassanian fire temples[59] and, of course, the combination of iwan and qubba had secular precedents well known to Islamic builders. The iwan had made a tentative appearance in the raising of the height of the central qibla bays of both the eastern and western court ranges in the late 9th-century mosque at Nayin (see 30, page 69). A century later at Niriz, it alone formed the sanctuary. At Zavareh by 1136 there was an iwan on each axis of a nearly square court, the one before the domed sanctuary on the qibla being much the largest.[60] A generation later the formula had

59 **Gulpayagan, Friday mosque** rebuilt from 1104, domed sanctuary.

The so-called kiosk type of mosque represented at Gulpayagan consists of a qubba adapted from the chahartaq of the Sassanian fire temple – indeed probably built on the site of a fire temple – by sealing the arch in the side facing Mecca with a mihrab but leaving the other three open to a precinct. Gulpayagan remained uncompromised by the addition of an iwan – unlike most others, including the mosque at Zavareh.

60 **Zavareh, Friday mosque** 1136.
The four-iwan formula appeared at Zavareh – originally a kiosk mosque – for the first recorded time. The main sanctuary iwan is as yet distinguished only by its size.

61 **Ardistan, Friday mosque** mid 12th century, court
seen from sanctuary iwan.

The precinct of a magnificent kiosk mosque, rebuilt
between 1072 and 1092 on the site of a fire temple, was
transformed into a court with four iwans c. 1160.

achieved superb monumentality in the conversion of the hypostyle mosque at Ardistan with two storeys of arcades between the four iwans.[61-62] At Isfahan, during these same years, four iwans were inserted in the Buyid Friday mosque and minarets further distinguished the frontispiece of the largest one, on the qibla before the sanctuary.[63-64] There the hypostyle hall had already been transformed by Nizam al-Mulk with the interpolation of a domed qubba of exceptional grandeur. Shortly after, a similar qubba was added to the north by his rival Taj al-Mulk, apparently as a grand entrance to the complex.

Brick was the usual material for structure and decoration in Seljuk Iran and neighbouring areas. Perishable units, not naturally cohesive, bricks need massing to sustain heavy loads but may easily be moulded with, or laid in, decorative patterns. Thus the piers at Isfahan were doubtless always stout but must have needed even greater girth when the original wooden roof was replaced with a domical vault over each bay after the fire of 1122.[65] Many of these

62 **Ardistan, Friday mosque** interior of qubba with mihrab.

132

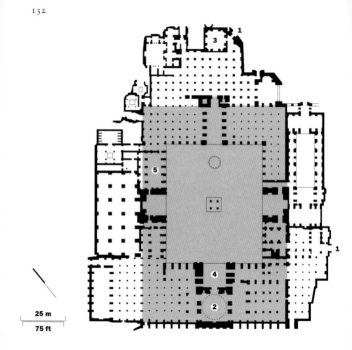

63 Isfahan, Friday mosque plan.

(Grey area) 10th-century Buyid court, hypostyle hall
and arcades probably extended into the court of an earlier
foundation – c. 140 by 90 metres (459 by 295 feet) – by
one bay all round; (1) public entrances; (2) qubba with
attributory inscription of Nizam al-Mulk (c. 1080);
(3) qubba with attributory inscription of Taj al-Mulk
(1088); (4) sanctuary iwan; (5) winter prayer hall (of the
Ilkhanid ruler Oljeitu?).

64 OVERLEAF Isfahan, Friday mosque court.

The date of the insertion of the iwans here is obscure,
but the main one is usually assigned to the second half of
the 12th century. If so, the earliest recorded example of twin
minarets applied to an iwan front (Ardistan, Imam Hasan
mosque, 1158) is roughly contemporary. Muqarnas vaults
appear in iwans by the 1130s (at Sin, for instance) but the
earliest here, those of the south iwan, were not inserted
until the second half of the 14th century and were reworked
a century later. Faience tiles solely in turquoise were used
to trace structural lines from the 11th century (at Damghan,
for instance) but coverage in multi-coloured tilework is
a phenomenon developed from the late 14th century at
the earliest.

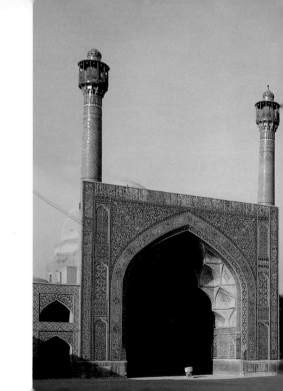

65 Isfahan, Friday mosque bays immediately to the east of the hypostyle hall, south of the entrance passage.

The date is unknown, but the combination of massive square and circular brick piers (rather than columns), plain or relieved with virile zig-zag patterns, accords with Buyid practice. The domical brick vaults which replaced the timber ceiling after a fire in 1122, echoed in later extensions to the prayer hall here and elsewhere, are notable for their variety.

domelettes are supported on muqarnas squinches and the great qubbas of Nizam al-Mulk and his rival[66] set the precedent in developing the theme first stated at Tim (see 36, page 77).

To supplement the decoration implicit in the brickwork, tile was inserted to enhance script or to articulate structural lines from the 11th century (see 64, pages 134–35). For special emphasis, particularly in the mihrab niche, stucco was carved into prominently relieved, highly stylised, sinuous and sensual floral patterns (see 62, page 130). The approach persisted well into the period of the Mongols, as in the mihrab of the Isfahani Friday mosque's winter prayer hall.[67–68]

66 OVERLEAF **Isfahan, Friday mosque** interior of northern qubba, 1088.

The qubba of Taj al-Mulk – originally freestanding to the north of the northern ranges of arcades – was probably the ceremonial entrance in the tradition of the domed ciborium. An inscription on the present oblique entrance to its east records rebuilding after the fire of 1122. The slightly earlier qubba of Nizam al-Mulk was possibly built as a maqsura, but immeasurably enhances the qibla.

In both these works – as elsewhere by the late 11th century – the zone of transition runs through eight to 16 arched sides, eight of them shallow squinches. In the main muqarnas squinches the tri-lobes of fragmentary vaulting are raised from the main walls of the cubical space by miniature façade elements, in which paired bays are framed by colonnettes supporting the fragments of vault, seeming to transmit the residual thrust of their arched profiles to a firm base. Inset in the massive walls, blind arches support the colonnettes at the confluences of the segments within each squinch. Between the squinches and the shallow side bays the colonnettes continue to the ground. The precision of the patterned brickwork is at its most impressive in the northern qubba. In the southern dome, ribs span straightforwardly between opposite corners of the octagon and the apexes of opposite arches, but the lattice of ribs forming a complex star in the northern dome demonstrates that the motif was decorative, not structural – though it may have been inspired by constructional procedure on a smaller scale.

67 **Isfahan, Friday mosque** winter prayer hall, dated
variously between the mid 14th and mid 15th centuries,
mihrab.

68 **Isfahan, Friday mosque** winter prayer hall.

Inserted to the north of the western iwan, the room is not uncommon in its vaulting, with a series of stout parallel transverse arches supporting pointed tunnel vaults. This technique for covering broad spaces in stone without intermediate supports, but allowing clerestory lighting, was familiar in Sassanian Iran. The most spectacular example from Oljeitu's era is the Han Ortmah at Baghdad.

Minars and mausoleums

Apart from the minarets attached to the sanctuary frontispieces of Friday mosques – as at Isfahan (see 64, pages 134–35) – Iran and its central Asian extension are well equipped with freestanding minars.[69] Not necessarily part of a mosque complex, their purpose is somewhat obscure but was probably multiple. Those near a Friday mosque were doubtless used to broadcast the times of prayer – but this alone does not explain their magnificence. As landmarks visible to the traveller from afar, announcing oases, they were monuments to the triumph of Islam above all – and to the glory of their patron.

As we have noted, towers were tombs too, but well before the end of the 11th century they were being eclipsed in Iran and its north-eastern extension into modern Afghanistan by the square or polygonal canopy type. The outstanding square example is the mid 12th-century tomb of Sultan Sanjar at Merv.[70]

69 **Bukhara, Kalayan minar** 1127.

Of exceptionally fine brickwork, but far less slender than the Seljuk norm in Iran, this great work was built by the Sultan Arslan Shah of the Qarakhanid dynasty.

70 **Merv, Tomb of Sultan Sanjar** 1157, plan and section.

Seventeen metres (56 feet) square with massive walls rising to 14 metres (46 feet) of unrelieved brickwork, it was covered by a semi-circular vault over which most reconstructions throw a separate helmet-shaped dome – an early example of a double-shell masonry dome, doubtless following a timber prototype, anticipated in one of the octagonal canopy tombs at Kharraqan (1093). Now lost except for the lower courses of brickwork, the outer shell of Sanjar's dome was covered with blue-glazed tiles. It rose from a drum, unlike the Samanid one at Bukhara (see 33–34, pages 74–75), but as there an arcaded gallery surmounts the main mass outside. At this level inside – the zone of transition – single-arched squinches enclosed rectangular windows with tri-lobed frames, and the tri-lobed pattern was echoed in the lower zone of the vault. The inner shell of the dome is relieved by a network of ribs running between every second and every fourth pier.

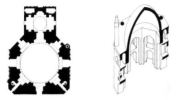

71 **Sultaniya, tomb of Oljeitu** c. 1310, plan and section.

Clearly inspired by the great Seljuk tomb at Merv –
and, ultimately, by the domed chambers at Isfahan (see 66,
page 139) – Oljeitu's architect goes further. The octagonal
plan naturally obviated the problem of effecting transition
from square to circle – and the versatility shown by the
Seljuks and their predecessors in designing squinches. Eight
great arches support an 'entablature' in which the cornice
consists of superimposed octagonal and circular rows of
muqarnas, masking the disparity between obtuse angle and
curve. Outside, the walls are relieved by largely blind arches
and the upper gallery subsists. The blue-glazed dome rises
from a shallow octagonal drum, invisible from below,
within the ring of eight minarets crowning the gallery.
Inside, glazed brick in contrasting tones of blue is far more
extensively used than previously, though painted plaster
was still important.

72 **Sultaniya,
tomb of Oljeitu**.

The outstanding example of the octagonal alternative, unprecedented in grandeur, is the tomb of the Ilkhanid ruler Oljeitu at Sultaniya in north-western Iran.[71-72] Sanjar's tomb, the earliest known to have been attached to a mosque, did not have a distinct façade, like the tomb at Tim (see 36, page 77). An entrance screen extended the full width of Oljeitu's octagon, but elsewhere – at Uzgend or Sarakhs in central Asia, for instance – the elaboration of the frontispiece theme first stated at Tim into a tall, slender façade suggests the synthesis of the canopy and tower tomb types.

The khanaqah

If not invariable, the pattern for the future of the mosque in Iran was set with the introduction of four iwans, and the formula ultimately found favour all over the Islamic world. The Ilkhanids furthered it, adding emphasis to the qibla axis by exaggerating the scale of the main iwan, covering the frontispiece more lavishly with tiles – as in the khanaqah of Sheikh Abd al-Samad at Natanz[73-74] – and incorporating twin minarets in the composition. Reflecting the organic development of the great shrines of the Shi'ite imams at the major Shi'ite pilgrimage centres, themselves

73 **Natanz, khanaqah of Sheikh Abd al-Samad** 1304
and after, entrance.

The khanaqah seems to have originated in eastern
Iran in the 10th century as the house of a mystic teacher
providing accommodation for his disciples (dervishes).
The Seljuks promoted the phenomenon in their challenge
to Shi'ism.

74 **Natanz, khanaqah of Sheikh Abd al-Samad** mosque with pyramidal tomb and minaret in the background.

In a way that was certainly not atypical of the Ilkhanid period, particularly at the great Shi'ite shrines, the mosque served as a madrasa. The tomb was perhaps originally a kiosk mosque converted for the purpose when the four-iwan one was built in 1304. The hostel, now lost except for its richly tiled frontispiece (restored), was added in 1317. The rich muqarnas are repeated over the entire vault inside.

largely rebuilt or re-embellished many times over later centuries, the accretion of prayer, teaching and hostel facilities around the tomb of a sufi saint was a common phenomenon even among the Sunnis.

Regional variations

Dozens of splendid mosques and madrasas, incorporating a court with or without the full complement of iwans, are to be found throughout the sphere of Seljuk activity. On the way from Iran, through Iraq to Anatolia, the Seljuks encountered an extraordinary mixture of competing forces, cultural and political. They pressed on, maintaining a presence in some of the towns, leaving the rest to local contenders whose monuments, naturally, betray wide-ranging influences. Most Iranian in the generally depressed area of northern Mesopotamia, claimed by the Kurds, is the great minaret of Mosul, all that remains of the mosque built by Nur al-Din Zengi.[75] Undoubtedly the most hybrid is the great mosque at Diyarbakr, with its Damascene plan, its Hellenistic Orders, its mixture of pointed arches and trabeated bays, and the vigour of Seljuk ornament translated from brick to stone.[76]

In Anatolia, the climate and the pervasive Byzantine

76 **Diyarbakr, great mosque** 1091, prayer-hall façade.

75 **Mosul, great mosque of Nur al-Din Zengi** before
1148 but possibly rebuilt later in the century, minaret.

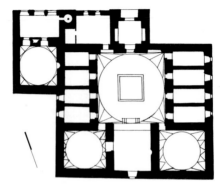

77 **Konya, Ince Minare madrasa** c. 1260, plan.

78 **Konya, Ince Minare madrasa** view towards entrance.
In addition to the type with an open court addressed by
one or more iwans, familiar in Seljuk domains elsewhere
and well represented by the Cifte Minare at Erzerum, the
Anatolian climate prompted the development of wholly
vaulted complexes. The domed hall of the Konya Ince
Minare, the most celebrated surviving example in the Rum

Seljuk capital, recalls the domed bema of the typical
Byzantine church, while the single iwan flanked by domed
chambers occupies the place of the sanctuary and its
flanking pastopheria. The Anatolian ratio of closed to
open space was often in reverse of the Mesopotamian and
Iranian norm: larger than the court, the prayer hall was
usually basilical.

Instead of the internal façade display provided by the
Iranian pishtaq, a magnificent entrance portal is embellished
with outstandingly vigorous stylised floral and geometric
motifs, knotted fillets and extraordinary interlaced bands of
Cufic script.

79 Erzerum, Cifte Minare madrasa 1253, plan.

With an open court, dominated by four iwans in the
Mesopotamian manner, the Erzerum madrasa is one of the
earliest in Anatolia to follow the Iranian Seljuk precedent of
incorporating two minarets in the frontispiece. At the other
end, beyond the qibla iwan, is a circular mausoleum with a
conical roof in the typical Anatolian Seljuk manner.

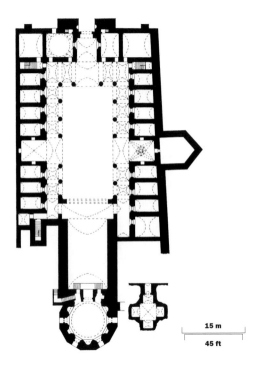

15 m

45 ft

80 **Erzerum, Cifte Minare madrasa** internal view
towards entrance.

tradition of the centralised church – perhaps recalling the early Iranian kiosk type of mosque to the immigrant Seljuks – prompted the development of the wholly domed mosque and madrasa as an alternative to the court and iwan type. In Rum, too, the Seljuks implanted the Iranian tower type of tomb, possibly derived from the tent (as we have noted) and echoed by the antique martyrium adapted by the Christians. The Ince Minare madrasa at Konya[77-78] and the Cifte

81 OVERLEAF **Kayseri, Doner Kumbed** c. 1275.

Derived from the Iranian tomb tower, but recalling the tent less equivocally than the earliest Iranian examples, the cylinder with its conical top is typical and has been related to the Armenian church tower – at least as much for the handling of the material as for the origin of the form. Stone was the usual building material in Anatolia, as in Armenia – but not, of course, in Iran. Apart from structural technique, it lent itself to the bold, exuberant, high-relief re-interpretation of Seljuk Iranian floral and Cufic brickwork mouldings and the addition of characteristically Armenian anthropomorphic and heraldic animal ones set within a light, even whimsical, architectonic frame and usually offset against extensive void. The result may best be

called grottesque in the sense the later Italian mannerists
were to give that word in designating the bizarre
combination of stylised structural, vegetal and even animal
motifs discovered in the cave-like remains of imperial
Roman interiors.

82 **Shivas, Gok madrasa** 1271, entrance front.

83 **Aleppo, al-Firdaus madrasa** 1235, court and iwan.
   The complex may have served the community for
communal prayers as well as providing facilities for
teaching. The mosque, on the southern side of the court
opposite the iwan, is a triple-domed hall. The iwan
addressing the court is backed by another facing north and
now unenclosed. Flanking the latter are two small courts,
each with at least two iwans.

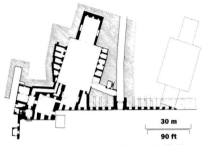

30 m

90 ft

84 **Cairo, tomb and madrasa of Sultan Salih Negm al-Din** 1241, plan.

The tomb of the last of the Ayyubids was associated with the first Cairene madrasa designed for the four branches of orthodox Sunni law. The Malikite and Shafi'ite schools were accommodated next to the tomb in a double-iwan court (modelled on the courtyard house as it had developed under the Fatimids). Across a small street to the south was an apparently identical (but now largely lost) double-iwan court for the Hanafites and Hanbalites. Both courts were flanked by cells on two storeys for the students, and a minaret crowns the entrance to both sides of the complex at the head of the intermediate street.

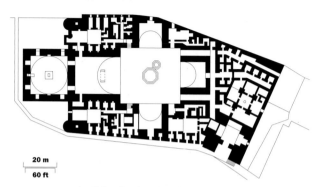

85 **Cairo, tomb and madrasa of Sultan Hasan** 1356, plan.

The four schools were accommodated in this complex, but the nuclear court primarily served a mosque, as in Iran, the four schools retreating from the iwans to the minor courts in the corners. As in the Friday mosque at Isfahan (see 63, page 132), the qibla iwan leads to a domed chamber: there it was a maqsura for the prince at prayer, here it is his tomb. The Cairene precedent for the four-iwan court scheme – minus the subsidiary courts – was set in the madrasa of Sultan al-Malik al-Nasir (1295–1303), the second ruler of the line which terminated with Sultan Hasan.

86 **Cairo, tomb and madrasa of Sultan Hasan** court.

87 **Cairo, tomb and madrasa of Sultan Hasan** iwan.

Ostentatious display was characteristic of the royal
funerary madrasas of Cairo, and the Hasan complex is
certainly no exception. Within the iwans of both court and
entrance (the latter originally conceived as a frontispiece
with paired minarets) muqarnas vaulting predominates.
Derived from Damascus (where it first appeared in the
mid 12th century), this type of vault first appeared in
Cairo shortly after the middle of the 13th century in the
Zahiriya madrasa of Sultan Baybars, ruler of Syria as well
as Egypt. Panelled revetment and voussoirs in marbles
of contrasting colours, surmounted by a frieze of bold
Cufic script, are common to several 13th-century Cairene
works. The precedent for Sultan Hasan's example was
the extraordinary complex of his ancestor Sultan Qala'un
(1280–90), whose tomb was set in a ring of columns
forming an octagon and circle within a square.

Minareli madrasa at Erzerum,[79-80] the latter incorporating a tent tomb like the Doner Kumbed at Kayseri,[81] represent the court and domed types respectively. Twin minarets appear over the iwan frontispiece, as in Iran,[82] and as in Iran the minaret is occasionally a free-standing monument.

The institution of the madrasa and the influence of the iwan on its planning – and on the planning of mosques – stretched well beyond the Seljuk sphere. Salah al-Din promoted the construction of madrasas in Egypt and Syria and his Ayyubid and Mamluk followers commissioned many splendid examples in both Cairo and Aleppo. The Egyptian rulers in particular endowed colleges in association with their tombs. The al-Firdaus madrasa in Aleppo[83] and the funerary complexes of sultans Salih Ngem al-Din[84] and Hasan in Cairo[85-87] may be taken as representative.

Secular building

After Samarra and Ukhaydir, the great palaces of the Abbasids and their Seljuk protectors have left little trace, though they were built to eclipse Ctesiphon – enough of which still stands in testimony to their failure. Throughout the area there are many great citadels

88 OVERLEAF **Cairo, citadel** 1271–82 and later, view
across the 'City of the Dead' with the mosque of
Muhammad Ali Pasha left and the domes and minarets
of the neighbouring al-Rifa'i and Hasan complexes right.

On its 200-metre (656-foot) eminence, dominating the
vast cemetery to the east of the Fatimid city and probably
fortified by the Romans, the citadel was refounded by
Salah al-Din as the key element in an extensive fortification
programme involving the construction of walls around
Fustat (the 'Entrenchment', the original Arab encampment
around which the first Muslim capital developed) and al-
Qahirah (the 'Vanquisher', the foundation of the Fatimid
conquerors as their new capital). The military zone to the
north-west preserves much of the original ramparts, with
their covered wall-walk and regular sequence of round
towers. The residential zone to the south-west has been
much enlarged. The palace, which reached its greatest
extent under Sultan al-Nasir Muhammad in the early 14th
century, consisted of many courts and pavilions, including a
throne chamber with a timber muqarnas vault preceded by a
many-columned portico commanding the magnificent view
of the city below. It was the best representative of many
generations of Cairene palaces until blown up in 1824, to
be replaced by the mosque of Muhammad Ali Pasha.

89 **Aleppo, citadel** late 12th century, walls and main gate.

Occupied since neo-Hittite times and a Muslim royal residence from the 10th century at least, Aleppo's present fortifications were founded by the late 12th-century Ayyubids and rebuilt by the Mamluks following the depredations of the Mongols in 1260. The ring of walls, punctuated by particularly stout bastions, is unrivalled in magnificence but typical in general form. The idea of projecting a major inhabitable mass over the gate, aggressively confronting the approach to the weakest point – and commanding the settlement beyond – was to be

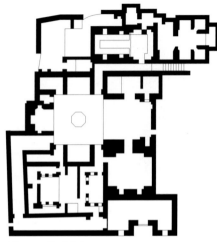

90 **Aleppo, citadel** plan.

further developed by both Muslim and Christian military
engineers. Projection of the machicolations in box-hoods
provided for the uninhibited patrol of sentries around the
enclosed wall-walks. This too became standard practice in
later defences throughout the Muslim and Christian world.

91 **Aleppo, citadel** portal of palace, c. 1233.

In the centre of the compound, at the top of its conical mound whose steep slopes formed an unscalable glacis, rather more than usual survives of the palace of Salah al-Din's early 13th-century successor, Sultan al-Malik al-Aziz Muhammad. An iwan with muqarnas led from the outer court, through a high wall of colourful masonry, to a circuitous passage which, in turn, led to the principal reception area. This consisted of a square atrium in the form of a roofed fountain court, with iwans to all four sides – the main one opposite the point of access.

and forts, and these usually do contain remnants of palaces.[88-91] For some idea of what the palaces of the post-Seljuk rulers of Syria were like, one may (with care) look well into the future and extrapolate.[92-93]

The Seljuks controlled much of the territory first amassed by the Achaemenids. That great domain was bound together by the best roads the world had yet seen, and over succeeding centuries imperial messengers and armies shared them with the caravans of traders – not least those who plied the so-called Silk Road to China. At intervals of a day's journey, these were accommodated in hostels (caravanserai). Defensible quadrangles related to both Roman fort and Mesopotamian palace in type, several of these date from the Seljuk period.[94-95] And in the towns which prospered on trade – never more than under the Seljuks – there were commodity exchanges for the wholesale distribution of goods[96] and covered shopping streets for the retailers.[97]

A major artery of power and commerce linked Mesopotamia and Iran to India through Afghanistan. The dynastic problems that had beset the Abbasids before the advent of the Seljuks and the destabilising rise of the Turks had ramifications in the east. Towards

92 **Damascus, Azem palace** 1749, fountain court and iwan.

93 **Damascus, Azem palace** circuitous entrance passage.

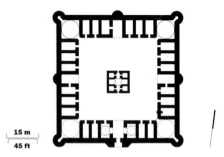

94 **Ribat-i Karim (north-west Iran), caravanserai**
c. 1100, plan.

Recalling the smaller enclosure of the Umayyad Qasr al-
Hayr al-Sharqi (see 16, page 42) – and beyond that the Roman
camp – this caravanserai is typical in its essentially defensive
blind walls punctuated by round towers, single entrance,
square court with central water tank, and four raised ranges
of cells for people and goods.

Originally designating a fort, the word *ribat* is sometimes
applied to the caravanserai since the latter was often
converted from the former. Strength through association is
implicit in the word *caravan*, but the domestic origin of the
type is perpetuated in the suffix *serai* (large house or
palace).

95 **Agzikara, han** c. 1230, court and mosque pavilion.
The Anatolian caravanserai are distinguished by the
centrally placed mosque (over the water tank) and the
basilican stable block attached to the court. Responding
to a climate which required cover even for the animals, like
the Anatolian form of wholly vaulted madrasa this was
influenced by the Christian church on the periphery of the
Byzantine empire (in Armenia in particular).

96 **Zavoreh, han** 14th century, interior.

Serving multiple purposes – exchange and public meeting place on festival days – this huge space is vaulted over a grid of stout piers rather than the transverse arches of structures like the winter prayer hall of the great Isfahani mosque (see 68, page 141) or the mid 14th-century Khan Mirjan in Baghdad.

97 **Yazd, souks** interior.

Comparatively modern, this colourful bazaar is typical and well represents a tradition at least as old as brick vaulting.

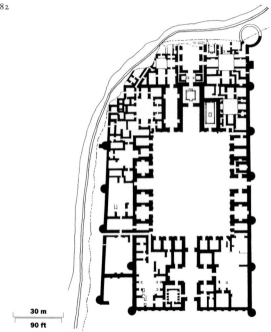

30 m
90 ft

98 **Lashkari Bazaar, palace** early 11th century, plan.

The so-called southern palace is one of several in a series of walled enclosures. In a rectangular compound – 100 by 250 metres (328 by 820 feet) – the distribution clearly recalls Samarra and Ukhaydir (see 21–22, pages 57–58) and beyond them Sassanian Firozabad and Parthian Assur (see volume 4, IMPERIAL SPACE, pages 98–103). The entrance hall (cruciform like several of the halls of Samarra) leads to a court with four iwans (as at Assur). As at Firozabad and Ukhaydir, the main one opposite the entrance leads to a domed room, a vestibule and a huge hall. To either side of this ceremonial core are four private suites – recalling Ukhaydir and the Umayyad paired apartments (see 16, page 42) – each with its own nuclear court and four iwans. The northern pair, accessible from the great hall, appear to have been the ruler's quarters. The one to the west of the main iwan, communicating with smaller courts and rooms added later to the west of the main court but with restricted access from it, was doubtless the harem quarters.

the end of the 10th century a Turkish slave raised a
rebellion against the Samanids in the eastern province
of Ghazni. His son, Mahmud, promoted the dynasty's
fall at the close of the century and founded his own.
He marked his triumph with ceremonial minars and
wielded power from the four-iwan courts of the
palaces at Ghazni and Lashkari Bazaar.[98]

Mahmud of Ghazni led his people in a series of raids
on the major religious centres of northern India in the
first three decades of the 11th century. They wanted
booty. A century and a half later, their Ghurid successors entered India with much more determined purpose.[99] But that marks the opening of a new chapter
in the history of Islam and its architecture.

99 **Jam, monumental minar of Ghiyas ud-Din** late 12th
century (19th-century engraving).

Way off on the western side of the Muslim world, there had been little stability in Morocco since the Berbers detected weakness in the Umayyads early in the 11th century. A chief of one of their nomadic clans, Yaha ibn Ibrahim, returned from pilgrimage to Mecca fired with puritan zeal, and quickly won a following. His successor, Yusuf ibn Tashufin, overawed southern Morocco and founded Marrakesh as the capital of his Almoravid dynasty in 1062. In 1069 he took Fez (see 46, page 96), still pre-eminent among the cities founded by the Arab colonists even after the passing of the Idrissids and the domination of Cordova. Pressing east into modern Algeria, he was to found Tlemcen in 1082.

Meanwhile the rivalry of the petty Arab and Berber states which had succeeded Cordova in Spain had proved disastrous for Islam. Ferdinand I of Castile (1037–65) had reduced Zaragoza, Toledo and even Seville to vassalage. His successor Alphonso VI annexed Toledo in 1085. The next year, in response to appeals from the beleaguered Muslims, Yusuf ibn Tashufin crossed to Spain, made a bridgehead at Valencia and went on to secure much of Andalucia. He died in 1107 and his fanatic energy died with him, but not before it had sapped the tolerance of the Christians. However, the culture of the conquered conquered the conquerors and sapped the will of his heir, Ali ben Yusef. By the end of his soft reign (1144), more Spanish Muslim states had been lost and the Moroccan tribes were restive again.

Another puritan sect, Berber tribal enemies of the Almoravids, set out from their rugged Atlas lair to extirpate corruption. They were led by yet another mahdi, Muhammad ibn Tumart, who returned from Mecca soon after Yusuf ibn Tashufin died and spent the rest of his life winning over other Berber tribesmen to unity with God. He died in 1130 but his equally zealous successor, Abd al-Mumin, took Marrakesh in 1141, Tlemcen in 1144, Fez in 1147 and assumed the title of caliph for his Almohad (unitarian) line. He then embarked on the conquest of Spain and Tunisia.

Abd al-Mumin's son Yusuf I (1163–84) established his court in Seville and devoted himself to scholarship and building. His son Yacob el-Mansour (conqueror) preferred his new camp in northern Morocco, Rabat. A sound ruler and great builder who was indeed a fine warrior, he pushed the frontier with Christianity back further and further north and consolidated his hold on north Africa. By the time of his death in 1199, the Moroccan empire had reached its greatest extent and the apogee of its glory. The triumph was cut short on the frontier with Castile by the Christian victory over el-Mansour's inadequate successor at the Battle of Las Navas de Tolosa in 1212. Cordova was Christian in 1236, Seville in 1248. By 1260 only the sultanate of Granada remained: that had been founded in 1238 by a descendant of the last king of Zaragoza and survived as a tributary of the king of Castile because he needed the revenue.

Fired by the quest for new pastures, rather than religious zeal, a hardy desert clan of Berbers took Fez in 1248 and made it the capital of their Marinid dynasty. Many other tribes were won over by vigour again. Marrakesh and the last of the Almohads fell in 1269. An expedition to Spain failed to rewin the old caliphate there, but close relations were forged with Granada. Tlemcen was retaken in 1336, but not Tunisia. Surviving until the mid 16th century, the Marinids devoted themselves to lavish building. Orthodox Sunni, if enlightened in their concern for public welfare, they promoted canonical education to counter

the heterodox radicalism and sufism which the zeal of
their predecessors had encouraged. The introduction
of the madrasa was their chief contribution to the
architecture of Morocco.

Moroccan builders

Iranian forms took longer to reach the far west. The
area was colonised largely by Arabs, as we have noted,
and Cordova's cultural predominance was long felt.
Fez was pre-eminent among Moroccan Arab towns,
and pre-eminent among Moroccan mosques is Fez's
Qarawiyin,[100] founded in 857 by an Arab immigrant
from Kairouan – whose name it perpetuates. Under
Umayyad domination by the mid 10th century, the

100   **Fez, Qarawiyin mosque** 850s, 950s, 1130s, court.

The original mosque, founded in 857, was 12 bays wide
and four deep. As at Kairouan (see 41–42, pages 86–88), there
was a minaret over the entrance to the court on axis with
the mihrab. Expansion for a growing population under the
Umayyads in the middle of the 10th century included four
new bays to either side, three new arcades to the north,
displacing the old court and minaret, and a new court
further north with a new minaret to its west, all in the still

relatively sober style of contemporary Cordova. Finally in
1134 the Almoravids moved the qibla wall three arcades
further south and enhanced the central axis with muqarnas
vaulting, interpenetrating arches and cannellated domelettes
in the late style of Cordova – indeed, craftsmen were
probably imported from Spain. Further Spanish-style
embellishment took place in the 16th century when the
courtyard was endowed with end pavilions and a central
frontispiece to the prayer hall.

mosque was renovated and expanded in the current
style of Cordova.

Under the spell of Andalucia, the Almoravid sultan
Ali ben Yusef further extended the mosque at Fez in
sympathy with the 10th-century Umayyad horseshoe
arcades and built new Friday mosques elsewhere.
Most of these have been rebuilt or ruined, but the
additions at Fez, the filigree mihrab-bay vault at
Tlemcen and the restored ablution-tank canopy
known as the Qubbat al-Barudiyin at Marrakesh[101]

101 Marrakesh, Friday mosque of Ali ben Yusof

c. 1120, ablution-tank canopy (Qubbat al-Barudiyin).

Supported on cusped and pointed horseshoe arches and
covered with a brick dome over a clerestory, the suspended
canopy vault takes the decorative abstraction of once
structural forms to its dazzling conclusion. Transition from
square within rectangle to cannelled dome within octagon
is effected through eight overlapping arches springing
between every second pier on adjacent sides, as in the
mihrab bay at Cordova (see 51, page 103). As there, cusped
and pointed horseshoe arches play their elaborate part in
squinches and windows, and putative muqarnas appear in
the corner zones.

are the dynasty's most spectacular surviving works. Muqarnas ramp over vaults and cornices. Horseshoe and cusped arches are wildly varied in profile. The decorative manipulation of structural form cedes little to late Cordova.

Puritan though they were, the Almohads were no less prolix in the embellishment of their mosques than the Almoravids. The mosque at Tinmal, the lair from which their mahdi Muhammad ibn Tumart and his disciple Abd al-Mumin set out, has extremely intricate muqarnas vaulting over the mihrab bay,[102] and the selective cusping of the prayer hall arches is unprecedented in convolution. The later rulers of the line emulated and surpassed the Almoravids' Mar-

102 **Tinmal, Friday mosque** 1035, outer mihrab bay.

The prayer hall has four arcades, nine bays wide, and the outer two bays extend as cloisters to the sides of the court. Forming a nave, the central bay is wider than the others and, as at Kairouan for instance (see 41, page 86), it joins a transept at right angles immediately in front of the mihrab. The arches are either of pointed horseshoe or extremely elaborate cusped forms. The mihrab bay has one of the earliest muqarnas domes in the west.

rakesh mosque in scale and commissioned a series of
minarets to mark their triumph in the old southern
capital of Morocco, in the new capital of Spain and
in the camp from which the empire was taken to its
greatest extent. Whereas bold geometry accompa-
nied the intricacy of Tinmal, ever more intricacy
alone relieved the bold towers of Marrakesh,
Seville[103] and Rabat. The whole gamut of Islamic

103 **Seville, Giralda minar** 1184.

Commissioned in 1172 by Yusuf I in emulation of the
Almoravid foundation in Marrakesh, the mosque consisted
of a relatively long, shallow court preceded by a 17-bay
prayer hall (now incorporated into the structure of one of
the world's largest cathedrals). Work on the great minar of
Marrakesh seems to have begun at the end of the previous
reign as part of the extension of the Almoravid mosque, that
at Seville in the last year of Yusuf's reign. The windows on
stepped levels at Marrakesh are framed in blind arches of
varied profile, cusped and interlaced at the top. Here the
motif of the interlaced arch is reduced to a delicate scale –
producing a two-dimensional version of muqarnas – and
extended in triple panels through most of the tower's height.
The top storey is Christian.

motifs relieves the gate of al-Mansur's Ouadiah Kasba at Rabat.[104]

The 13th century was not a great age of building in Morocco. Almohad ambitions ended with the death of el-Mansour in 1199. His inadequate successors were preoccupied with unsuccessful war in Spain and at home. Once firmly established after their protracted advent, however, the Marinids augmented many mosques and inaugurated a great campaign of madrasa building at Fez[105–107] with the translation of

104 **Rabat, Ouadiah Kasba** c. 1195, gate.

The entrance to the fort palace begun under Abd al-Mumin set the pattern for the ceremonial gate in Morocco and Muslim Spain. In the valance ringing the voussoir and the frieze, the motifs of the lobed and cusped arch – blind, small-scale and out of structural context again – are varied in profile as at Tinmal (see 102, page 195), and meshed as on the great minars of Marrakesh, Seville (see 103, page 197) and (slightly later) Rabat. Stylised floral motifs and scallop shells fill the spandrels within the frame of Cufic script. The whole repertory of Islamic decorative forms is present, if geometry is admitted as the generator of the meshed lobed arches.

105 **Fez, Attarine madrasa** 1323, view towards qibla.

The court is rectangular, with the dog-leg entrance and square prayer hall on the short southern and northern sides respectively. This means that the mihrab marking the qibla is off-axis in the hall's right-hand wall. Of the other iwans, the southern one leads from the dog-leg passage (a typical domestic ploy to preserve privacy), but those on the eastern and western sides merely accent the arcades of shallow cloisters that flank the court throughout its length. Over a dado of coloured tiles set in simple geometric patterns, pilasters, walls and the screens that fill the arches above the northern and southern cloisters are covered with ornament incised in wood and stucco. The cusped-arch motif still plays a predominant role, but now it is repeated through several planes to resemble muqarnas – mirror-imaged to form a diaper pattern – or interlaced with such convolution that it is hardly to be distinguished from stylised floral ornament. Floral ornament has its role too, as does script.

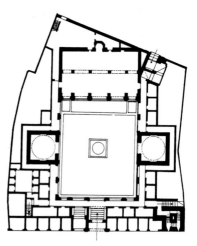

106 **Fez, Bou Inaniya madrasa** 1350, plan.

As elsewhere by the mid 14th century, the four-iwan madrasa doubles as a mosque here. The site was about half way between the Qarawiyin mosque in the centre of the old town and the new Maranid seat of Fez al-Jedid (founded 1276). Pending the construction of a new congregational mosque in the new town, the Bou Inaniya served the

107 **Fez, Bou Inaniya madrasa** prayer-hall façade.

The integration of wood, stone and plaster still provides the basis for the profuse embellishment of the court façades.

purpose and was endowed with the city's tallest minaret. The entrance, court and mosque are aligned canonically on the qibla. The iwans on the other two sides open into teaching halls. Two storeys of cells for up to 100 students are served by corridors in the corners, except to the north-east, and shops mask the exterior to either side of the central entrance (where a water clock measures the time for prayer).

the iwan into Moroccan terms. There were to be many variants on awkward sites in the tight context of Morocco's cities but all tend to be plain on the outside, profusely ornamented around the court, and plain again inside except for the vault and mihrab of the mosque.[108]

108 **Marrakesh, madrasa of Ibn Yusuf** rebuilt 1562 on a Marinid foundation, mihrab.

More regular in its disposition than was the norm – indeed near symmetrical in a nearly square compound – the last of the great Moroccan madrasas grouped the cells of the students on two floors around seven internal courts rather than along corridors, though access to them was gained along corridor-like galleries on three sides of the court. The entrance corridor, at right angles to the court iwan which opens the qibla, occupied the place where the eighth court might have been.

The lack of exuberance in the court façade embellishment suggests tired tradition, rather than new-found moderation under the Saadian successors to the Marinids, but the emphasis on the mihrab perpetuates the most sumptuous of Islamic decorative traditions. Later dynasties continued the lavishness, the Saadians (1554–1660) further refining it.

The Alhambra

Surprisingly, perhaps, the new-found intolerance with which the Christians confronted the once zealous Almohads did not extend to the so-called Moorish style – indeed, they furthered it in the Alcazar palace in Seville.[109] And under the sufferance of Castile, the sultans of Granada luxuriated in the extreme prolixity of the Alhambra. On its splendid site, in its stoutly defended compound, beyond the extreme beauty of its

109 **Seville, Alcazar** throne room.

An extensive Moorish palace complex survives in the Seville Alcazar, but much of it was rebuilt (or at least redecorated) by the Christian king Pedro the Cruel in the second half of the 14th century. The extent to which the nucleus represents the Almohads is controversial, but the Yeso court – with an iwan in the variegated cusped style of Tinmal (see 102, page 195) and later Almohad structures – is usually accepted and the disposition of the rooms around the Court of the Maidens may well prefigure, rather than follow, the Alhambra. The throne room has a splendid ceiling patterned with intricate inlaid and overlaid wooden beams and panels. The type, called *artesonado*, was popular with Moorish patrons.

courts and terraces, this legendary work is of prime
importance because the extent of its preservation is
unique among the palaces of Islam.

In the packed confines of a citadel, the traditional
tripartite division is far from dogmatic[110] – there is,
indeed, nothing dogmatic about this fantasy palace.
Presumably the missing outer courts were for public
audience – or at least for public assembly in atten-
dance on the ruler. Likewise, at the other end of the
sequence, some of the harem quarters and the pala-
tine mosque disappeared under the church and palace
of Charles V. Of the wonderful array of courts and
halls whose survival is the more miraculous given

110 **Granada, Alhambra** plan.

(1) Outer court; (2) mosque; (3) Court of Machuca;
(4) Mexuar; (5) Cuarto Dorado and its court; (6) Court
of the Myrtles; (7) Hall of the Ambassadors; (8) baths;
(9) Court of the Lions and halls of (10) the Two Sisters,
(11) the Abencerajes, (12) Justice; (13) Muqarnas. Beyond
the Court of the Lions and its surrounding rooms are
gardens which once served the harem (destroyed for the
construction of the palace of Charles V). The complex is
completed and extended to the neighbouring hill by gardens

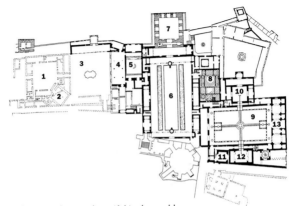

which rank among the most beautiful in the world.

The site was occupied in Roman times. The 9th-century foundations, overlaying the Roman ones, are themselves overlaid by the remains of the palace built in the middle of the 11th century by a Jewish vizier. Fortifications dependent on a massive keep on the western point of the site (the Alcazaba) and services (particularly an aqueduct) were built by the first Grenadine sultans, Muhammad I and II, in the 13th century and work was begun on the outer courts (now mainly gone).

their extreme delicacy, the Court of the Myrtles[111] catered for the grandest semi-public functions designated by its dependant Hall of the Ambassadors. The Court of the Lions,[112] with its dependant halls of private audience, was the heart of the ruler's personal quarters, communicating directly with the harem. As privacy increases so does the refinement of the full repertory of motifs inherited from the Almohads and

111 **Granada, Alhambra** Court of the Myrtles.

The ceremonial nucleus of the Court of the Myrtles and its dependancies was developed in the pre-existing tower known as al-Qamariya by Yusuf I (1333–54), who also built the parade entrance, the Gate of Justice – which recalls the venerable place of appearance of rulers from ancient Mesopotamia to Rome and Byzantium.

112 OVERLEAF **Granada, Alhambra** Court of the Lions.

The Court of the Lions and its dependancies were arranged by Muhammad V (1354–59 and 1362–91) around the fountain which provides the name (itself surviving from the palace of the Jewish vizier and probably inspired by the great bowl on 12 oxen in the Temple of Solomon at Jerusalem).

ultimately the Umayyads of Cordova – indeed, the muqarnas ceilings of the innermost halls know no equal in their exquisite intricacy.[113]

The complex marks a new apogee for the ubiquitous courtyard house – if the fabulous villa built for the emperor Hadrian at Tivoli marked the first, the Byzantine imperial palace at Constantinople another and the Jusaq al-Khaqani at Samarra (see 21, page 57) yet another. At Tivoli, at least (see volume 4, IMPERIAL SPACE, page 44), the site permitted the loose devolution of intrinsically formal units. Here, the tightly packed confines of an acropolis on the one hand, its splendid elevation on the other, inspired a cantilena of expansive outlook[114–115] played in counterpoint over a ground base of intense introversion. And it is in contemplating the most seductive Court of the Lions that the full meaning of the exercise is revealed. With its central fountain and crossed canals, it is an image of Eden's lost paradise regained. At first the rectangle seems to deny this, for the ancient Persian *pradaieza*, from which Eden springs, is a square divided by the

113 **Granada, Alhambra** Hall of the Two Sisters, muqarnas vault.

114 **Granada, Alhambra** Cuarto Dorado.

The Cuarto Dorado and its court were added early in
the 14th century by Muhammad III and decorated under
Yusuf I. The hall of the Cuarto Dorado is one of the main
outward-looking belvederes.

115 OVERLEAF **Granada, Alhambra** harem gardens and
pavilion.

The immediate precedents for the Alhambra and its
Marinid predecessors – which are known from literary
accounts to have been similar, if grander – were set by the
Almohads in Seville. The Almohads doubtless followed
the now lost example of the metropolitan palace of the
Cordovan caliphs. We have already noted the sensitivity to
site in the arrangement of courts and terraces in the retreat
of Abd al-Rahman III at Medinat al-Zahira (see 52, page 106);
somewhat later and considerably further east, in north-east
Algeria, the early 12th-century Qasr al-Mulk of the Banu
Hammad similarly combines major formal courtyard
complexes, related in plan to various Umayyad, Abbasid
and even Ghaznavid precedents, in informal agglomeration
– recalling the sensitivity to site contours of Hadrian's villa.

116 **Granada, Generalife gardens** canal.

117 **Granada, Generalife gardens**.

rivers of life into the four quarters of creation. But the arms of the canals are in fact co-extensive and in their penetration through the iwans of the axial pavilions – projecting into the court east and west, receding from it north and south – is the literal interpretation of the Koranic paradise as a garden set with pavilions beneath which water flows. The cantilena takes up the theme and varies it with infinite resource.[116–118]

118 **Granada, Generalife gardens** view from belvedere back to the Alhambra.

glossary

AEDICULE ornamental niche to house a sacred image, for example.

AISLE side passage of a BASILICA or temple, running parallel to the NAVE and separated from it by COLUMNS or PIERS.

AMBULATORY semi-circular or polygonal arcade or walkway.

APSE semi-circular domed or vaulted space, especially at one end of a BASILICA.

AQUEDUCT artificial channel or conduit for water.

ARCADE series of arches supported by COLUMNS, sometimes paired and covered so as to form a walkway.

ARCHITRAVE one of the three principal elements of an ENTABLATURE, positioned immediately above the CAPITAL of a COLUMN, and supporting the FRIEZE and CORNICE.

ARCUATE shaped like an arch. Hence (of a building) arcuated, deploying arch structures (as opposed to TRABEATED).

ARTESONADO type of wooden ceiling in Spanish Islamic building, with intricate patterns of carved beams and panels.

ATRIUM entrance hall or courtyard, usually open to the sky.

BAGH garden.

BASILICA temple or other public building, consisting principally of a COLONNADED rectangular space enclosed by an AMBULATORY or having a central NAVE and side AISLES, often with an APSE, and generally lit by a CLERESTORY.

BASTION structure projecting from the angle of a defensive wall, enabling enhanced vision and mobility for a garrison.

BATTERING reinforcement of wall bases by building a sloping supporting structure.

BAY one of a series of compartments of the interior of a building, the divisions being created by PIERS or COLUMNS, for example.

BEAM horizontal element in, for instance, a TRABEATED structure.

BEIT paired apartments characteristic of Umayyad domestic building. (See page 42.)

BELVEDERE open-sided roofed structure, freestanding or situated on the roof of a building so as to command a view.

BEMA sanctuary of a church, especially Byzantine.

BIT-HILANI columned PORTICO, originally of 1st millennium BC Syria.

CANNELLATED channelled or fluted.

CAPITAL top part of a COLUMN, supporting the ENTABLATURE.

CARAVANSERAI enclosure providing overnight accommodation for travellers; usually square, related to and sometimes interchangeable with RIBAT. (See page 178.)

CARDO road running north to south, later the principal longitudinal road of a town or city.

CENOTAPH funerary monument remote from the location of the remains of those commemorated.

CHAHAR-BAGH formal garden, ideally square and divided into four smaller squares by axial paths or canals.

CHAHAR-TAQ square domed structure characteristic of Zoroastrian fire temples, and adapted for use in other circumstances.

CIBORIUM canopy raised on columns so as to form a covering above an altar or tomb.

CITADEL fortress, usually at the highest part of a town.

CLERESTORY windowed upper level providing light for a double-storey interior.

CLOISTER covered ARCADE, often running around the perimeter of an open courtyard.

COLONNADE line of regularly spaced COLUMNS.

COLONNETTE small COLUMN, decorative and/or functional.

COLUMN vertical member, usually circular in cross-section, functionally structural or ornamental or both, usually comprising a base, shaft and CAPITAL.

CONCRETE building material composed of cement agglomerated with sand, gravel, stone chippings, et cetera.

CORBEL course of masonry or support bracket, usually stone, for a BEAM or other horizontal member. Hence corbelled: forming a stepped roof by deploying progressively overlapping corbels.

CORNICE projecting moulding forming the top part of an ENTABLATURE. More generally, a horizontal ornamental moulding projecting at the top of a wall or other structure.

CUFIC SCRIPT originating in Cufa in Iraq,

a stylised form often features in Islamic painting and carving.

CUSP projection formed between two arcs, especially in stone tracery, hence CUSPED. (See page 64.)

DADO the middle part, between base and CORNICE, of a PEDESTAL, or the lower part of a wall when treated as a continuous pedestal.

DAR AL-IMARA regional governor's palace and/or administration centre.

DECUMANUS road running east to west, later the main latitudinal road of a town or city.

DIAPERWORK repeated pattern in brick or tile, for instance, often involving diamond shapes.

DOMELETTE small dome, decorative and/or functional.

ENTABLATURE part of the façade immediately above the COLUMNS, usually composed of a supportive ARCHITRAVE, decorative FRIEZE and projecting CORNICE.

FAIENCE type of glazed earthenware.

FASTIGIUM a PEDIMENT or other structure in the shape of the gable end of a house, dignifying the entrance to a temple precinct or palace.

FILIGREE decorative work formed from a mesh or by piercing material to give the impression of a mesh.

FILLET top part of a CORNICE, or generally a decorative moulding in the shape of a narrow raised band.

FORUM central open space of a town, usually a marketplace surrounded by public buildings.

FRIEZE the middle part of an ENTABLATURE, above the ARCHITRAVE and below the CORNICE, or more generally any horizontal strip decorated in RELIEF.

FRONTISPIECE principal entrance and its surround, usually distinguished by decoration and often standing proud of the façade in which it sits.

GLACIS slope or ramp in front of, for instance, a defensive wall.

HAN relatively small, usually urban, inn or CARAVANSERAI.

HAREM women's quarters.

HAZARBAF type of ornate brickwork.

HYPOSTYLE HALL hall with a roof supported by numerous COLUMNS, more or less evenly spaced across its area.

IMPOST structural member – usually in the form of a MOULDING or block – at the top of a pillar, for instance, on which an arch rests.

INTERCOLUMNIATION the space between two columns, often expressed as a multiple of column diameters.

IWAN vaulted hall or recess opening off a court.

KHANAQAH type of building providing accommodation and study quarters for sufi disciples.

KIOSK small open pavilion, often pillared.

KORAN the book of law governing the practice of the Muslim religion.

LINTEL horizontal member over a window or doorway or bridging the gap between two COLUMNS or PIERS.

LOBE projection formed between two arcs, especially in stone tracery; larger form of CUSP. (See page 64.)

MACHICOLATION gallery or parapet projecting on CORBELS from the outside of defensive walls, with holes for missiles to be dropped or thrown.

MADRASA Islamic school or college generally associated with a MOSQUE.

MAQSURA the area in a mosque within which the caliph worshipped: also the protective screen enclosing that area.

MARTYRIUM shrine or chapel dedicated to Christian martyrs.

MAUSOLEUM tomb, usually of a dignitary, built on a grand scale.

MIHRAB niche or marker in a MOSQUE indicating the direction of Mecca.

MINAR freestanding monumental tower, usually used to call Muslims to the MOSQUE to prayer. (See page 142.)

MINARET tower attached to a MOSQUE, from which Muslims are called to prayer.

MINBAR type of pulpit in a MOSQUE, usually consisting of a small dais with a throne, reached by steps.

MOSAIC decoration formed by embedding small coloured tiles or pieces of glass in cement.

MOSQUE Muslim temple/complex.

MOULDING the contour of a projecting or inset element.

MUQARNAS miniature SQUINCH form used in combination functionally in effecting transition from, for instance, polygonal chamber to domed roof; and/or used decoratively to produce a honeycomb effect.

NAVE central body of principal interior of, for instance, a BASILICA.

NICHE recess in a wall, often containing a statue.

PARAPET low wall, usually for defensive purposes.

PASTOPHERIA in the Byzantine church, areas to the sides of the rear of the sanctuary used by priests for preparations for ritual.

PAVILION lightly constructed building, often tent-like and set in a garden.

PEDESTAL base supporting a COLUMN or statue.

PIER supporting pillar for wall or roof, often of rectangular cross-section.

PILASTER a PIER of rectangular cross-section, more or less integral with and only slightly projecting from the wall which it supports.

PISHTAQ a FRONTISPIECE or monumental PORTAL standing proud of the façade of a building.

PLINTH rectangular base or base support of a COLUMN or wall.

PORTAL doorway, usually on a grand scale.

PORTICO entrance to a building, featuring a COLONNADE.

POST vertical element in, for instance, a TRABEATED structure.

PROPYLAEUM gateway, especially to a temple enclosure.

QUADRANGLE rectangular courtyard surrounded on all sides by ranges of buildings.

QIBLA orientation of a MOSQUE such that prayer is directed towards Mecca: also, of a mosque, the wall that faces towards Mecca.

QUBBA domed cubical chamber with open sides.

RAMPART defensive earthwork, usually surrounding a fortress or citadel, often with a stone PARAPET.

RELIEF carving, typically of figures, raised from a flat background by cutting away more (high relief) or less (low relief) of the material from which they are carved.

REVETMENT decorative reinforced facing for a wall.

RIB raised band on a VAULT or ceiling.

RIBAT fortified enclosure, usually square, associated with Muslim holy warriors.

RIWAQ shelter, usually in a MOSQUE, consisting of an ARCADE open on one side.

ROTUNDA circular room or building, usually with a domed roof.

SCENAE FRONS flat wall forming the back of the stage in a semi-circular Roman theatre.

SERAI palace.

SOUK market, often contained within a covered ARCADE.

SPANDREL triangular space formed by the outer curve of an arch and the horizontal and vertical elements of the rectangle within which the arch sits.

SQUINCH arch placed across the corner of a square structure so as to form a polygon capable of being roofed by a dome.

STUCCO type of plaster, especially used where decoration is to be applied.

TEMENOS sacred enclosure, usually adjacent to a temple.

TETRAPYLON four columns surmounted by a PLINTH, or monumental arch with intersecting passages, used to mark the junction of major roads in a Roman town.

TRABEATED structurally dependent on rectilinear POST and BEAM supports.

TRANSEPT part of a large public/religious building that crosses the NAVE at right angles.

TURRET small tower, often at the angle of a building.

VAULT structure forming an arched roof.

VAULT, BARREL enclosing a more or less hemicylindrical space.

VAULT, CANOPY creating a roof for a NICHE or tomb.

VAULT, TUNNEL enclosing a more or less hemicylindrical space.

VERANDAH roofed COLONNADE attached to one or more sides of a building.

VIHARA residential quarters of a Buddhist monastery.

VOUSSOIR wedge-shaped stone deployed in building an arch. Hence voussoir arch, where such stones are used.

ZIGGURAT building usually composed of a stepped series of concentric rectangles, the whole forming a truncated pyramidal structure.

The books listed below are those the author found particularly useful as sources of general information on the architecture covered in this volume.

Ettinghausen, Richard and Grabar, Oleg, *The Art and Architecture of Islam 650–1250*, Harmondsworth 1987
Creswell, K A C, *Early Muslim Architecture*, 2 volumes, Oxford 1932 and 1940
Hillenbrand, Robert, *Islamic Architecture*, Edinburgh 1994
Hoag, J, *Islamic Architecture*, London 1975

Sources of illustrations
pages 30, 57, 163, 202, 209 J Hoag, *Islamic Architecture*, London 1975; pages 42, 123, 157, 182 R Ettinghausen and O Grabar, *The Art and Architecture of Islam 650–1250*, Harmondsworth 1987; page 106 R Hillenbrand, *Islamic Architecture*, Edinburgh 1994; page 111 Madrid, Museo Arqueológico Nacional (photo museum)

bibliography

index

This 25-volume series tells the story of architecture from the earliest settlements in the Euphrates and Jordan valleys to the sophisticated buildings of the late twentieth century. Each volume sets the buildings described and illustrated within their political, social, cultural and technological contexts, exploring architecture not only as the development of form but as an expression of the civilisations within which it evolved. The series focuses on the classical tradition from its origins, through its seminal realisation in ancient Greece and Rome, to the Renaissance, neo-classicism, eclecticism, modernism and post-modernism, supplemented with excursions to India and south-east Asia.

CHRISTOPHER TADGELL teaches architectural history at the Kent Institute of Art and Design and has lectured widely in Britain and the USA.

VOLUMES I TO 9

••• **a history of architecture** christopher tadgell **7**

four empires of islam
imperial achievement

At the end of the 12th century, Islam dominated a swathe of the then-known world, from Spain to India, with outposts along the Silk Road trade route to China. *Four Empires of Islam* traces Islamic architecture's development from Timur's 14th-century empire to the Ottomans.

Timur built mosques and madrasas using architects and craftsmen from all over the empire. Their form was generally traditional, the scale unprecedented. Apart from the decorative elaboration of structural forms, colour and pattern were increasingly used to reinforce structural lines.

In Mughal India, a synthesis of traditional forms and those imported from Persia produced a magnificent series of mosques, citadels, and tombs, including the Taj Mahal, the apotheosis of the Muslim tradition.

The Ottomans, who on taking Constantinople converted Hagia Sophia to a mosque, embarked on a series of variations on its plan, embracing centralisation to assert the boundless expansion of Islamic faith in the centrifugal aspiration of mass and space.